# MIND GAMES

# MIND GAMES

*Robert Masters and Jean Houston*

**DORSET PRESS**
New York

This edition published by Dorset Press,
a division of Marboro Books Corporation,
by arrangement with the
Roslyn Targ Literary Agency, Inc.
1989 Dorset Press


Acknowledgment is made to
Dover Publications, Inc., for illustrations from
*Optical and Geometrical Patterns and Designs*
by Spyros Horemis.
Copyright © 1970 Dover Publications, Inc.


ISBN 0-88029-447-7


Printed in the United States of America

M 9 8 7 6 5 4 3 2 1

*These books of mind games are dedicated to*

ARTHUR AND PRUE CEPPOS

## Acknowledgments

The mind games were tested, and most of them devised, by the authors in the course of experimental work at The Foundation for Mind Research. However, a few of the games included in this book were suggested to the authors by experiments and other works of Bernard Aaronson, Martha Crampton, John C. Lilly, Abram Hoffer, and Humphry Osmond. A larger indebtedness is to the published work and example of Milton H. Erickson.

Special thanks are due Alice O'Donnell, whose consciousness was a testing ground for the ordering and verbalizing of the games as they are set forth in the books.

# Contents

*Mind Games:* **BOOK ONE**

# *A Special Note to Mind-Games Players:*

It is essential that the mind games be played in the order given.

This means that the players must begin the first game in Book One, and complete the Book One games in order before moving to Book Two.

And the Book Two games must then be completed in order before going to Book Three, and Book Three games completed in order before going on to Book Four.

The order of the games has been carefully thought out, on the basis of a great deal of experience. This order has the function of training and preparing the players for games of ever-increasing richness, depth, and complexity.

The rewards will not be the same for players who deviate from the given structure as they will be for players who follow it. Those who attempt, for example, to begin with some of the Book Three or Book Four games will have at best diluted, impoverished experiences as compared to those who have laid the essential ground-work by passing through the preceding games as given in the books.

*About mind games:*

Mind games anticipate the play-learning systems of the future, opening that future to you *now*.

Mind games are education, ecstasy, entertainment, self-exploration, powerful instruments of growth.

Those who play these games should become more imaginative, more creative, more fully able to gain access to their capacities and to use their capacities productively.

The players should achieve a new image of man as a creature of enormous and unfolding potentials.

The players should become increasingly hopeful that the powers of the human being are sufficient to deal with the problems that confront us.

The players should emerge from these games convinced that man is not something we know has to be surpassed; rather, man is still something to be realized.

And the mind games are a means of advancing toward what must be the main goal of every person in our time—
*putting the first man on the earth.*


*Background of the games:*

The games are products of research—the research of the authors and also, in some instances, of other persons. We have played these games or similar games with research subjects and friends for many years.

The average person is able to play, and to benefit from playing. Research has proved this, as it has proved that the mind games do really work.

*Preparations for playing:*

First of all, read through this "Book One," and through the "Guide's Book for Mind Games." Better, read through all five of the books which together make up this volume.

Discuss the books and the playing of mind games with persons who will be playing the games with you.

Resolve any major doubts or anxieties you have before beginning to play the games. Never participate in any game if you feel strongly that you should not.

Play with the aim of gaining self-knowledge, of liberating some of your potentials, of learning to use your mind-brain system much more effectively than you have been able to do.

Play to have rich and novel experiences.

Play for pleasure as well as for enlightenment and more effective use of your capacities.

Some of the best human experiences happen when work and play are one.

*Setting and players:*

A few practical details will be given here in this first volume of the game books. But the "Guide's Book" also must be read.

The setting of the games, whether indoors or out, should be comfortable and made free of unwanted distractions.

For example, telephone calls and visitors are not compatible with the playing of the mind games. Consider the game you are going to play and select the best setting available.

In general, play mind games only with persons you trust, are comfortable with, and have come to know fairly well. This precaution will enrich the experiences of all players, making it easier for each player to let go of conditioned behaviors and ways of perceiving and knowing. One mistrusted, hostile, exploitative, or otherwise objectionable player may greatly diminish the experience of other persons or of an entire group.

*The player who is guide:*

All of the mind games require that one or more of the players assume the role of "guide."

The guide should be a person who communicates well, who is a good practical psychologist, and who is able by performance to demonstrate to the satisfaction of the players that she or he is competent to guide.

It is best if eventually most if not all members of a group fulfill the guide's role. In this way, as many players as possible have a chance to develop guiding skills. And the group is less likely to become concerned with questions of authority or other conflicts related to dominance or controversial exercise of power. The "Guide's Book" goes into detail about guide selection and rotation.

The performance of the guide should be recognized as being of great importance, very strongly affecting how the games will be experienced by the players.

The guide is the enabler, the one who helps the players to turn on, to let go, to break free from the limitations of everyday seeing, feeling, and thinking—from old ways of being.

Sometimes it may be required of the guide that he or she give comfort to a player, or a considerable amount of direction. But the best guide is the least obtrusive one, the one who does what is needed but also leaves each player free to have her or his own experience.

When the game has been played, the player should have little awareness of the skillful, subtle guidance that was given. And the guide should not want it to be otherwise.

The guide also assists the players' re-entry, so that each player ends each mind game refreshed, energized, leaving nothing of value behind, bringing back something of value to enrich the group and the general reality consensus.


*Altered States of Consciousness (ASCs):*

Mind games alter consciousness and altered states of consciousness (ASCs) facilitate and enrich the mind games.

ASCs=expanded possibilities for mind.

ASCs=deconditioned, deautomatized mind-brain system.

ASCs disinhibit, give access to new experiences, ordinarily unused and largely unusable capacities.

For example, images, accelerated mental process, more

acute sense impressions, access to other places of the mind, subjective realities, new space-time orientations.

The guide helps the players to open inner doors, gateways to the other places within, and after that accompanies the player and returns with the player when the voyage is over. And closes the door to the other places after guide and player have passed back through again into the embarkation area.

The guide is most active during entry and re-entry, during the opening and closing of the doors, and the guide also will assign tasks or outline areas to be explored. But apart from these functions, the experience of a player should be intruded upon as little as possible.

There are many ways of opening the doors, and it is easy to do if the guide is effective and all players choose and are able to cooperate. It is enough for the guide just to talk for a while, with the players responding to what the guide says to them.

Later, as the players experience and learn, players will be able to open their own doors, induce their own ASCs, and the guide will only need to ask them to do that.

*Opening the doors:*

There are many ways of opening the doors, and of doing this just by talking, and the following key or induction procedure will be used by the guide when the first mind game is to be played, and from time to time thereafter. And the guide will begin by requesting of the players that they pay close attention to suggestions about relaxing, about letting go of body-mind tensions. The guide might say, for example:

Make yourself very comfortable now, relaxing just as fully as you can, and now listen closely and discover that you can relax still more.

Relax your body a bit at a time, beginning with the toes, just let them go very limp and relaxed. Then the rest of the foot, and the ankle, feeling the ankle going limp and relaxed, and that relaxation moving up through your body, to the calves, and the knees, and on up to the thighs, and just going very, very limp in your body as I describe the progression of this deep relaxation to you.

And now on up into the pelvic area, relaxing, relaxing, more and more relaxed. And the abdomen now, and on up to the chest, going loose and limp all over. The fingers, the wrists, the forearms, the elbows, upper arms, and on up to the shoulders now, feel the relaxation, all strain or tension slipping out and away from your whole body. So that the neck feels so loose and limp now, and the jaw, the lips, the cheeks, and the eyes, right on up to the forehead, and over the entire head.

The entirety of your body relaxed now, and relaxing even more and more, so that you are just as limp and relaxed as an old rag doll appears to be, and you really are that relaxed, as you listen now to what I have to say to you, and you will want to listen extremely closely, very, very closely please, as you are listening just to me, becoming aware just of what is said to you, and of your responses to what is being said to you.

And for a little while now, with closed eyes, remaining relaxed, breathing slowly and deeply, focus your awareness on that breathing, as you breathe in now, and then breathing out ... in and out, in and out, in and out....

After about two minutes of this, with the players breathing in and out as suggested, the guide might begin a more potent ASC induction, knowing that each player is going to respond differently, some more profoundly than others, but that all players are learning to respond, preparing the way for an ever more complete participation in the mind games. And the guide then would say:

Let your eyes remain closed now, be deeply relaxed, and there is something of importance and value to you that I have to say to you now.

So concentrate just upon what I will say to you, very fully concentrated on my words, and on what you will experience when the words are spoken. Remember, and accept without doubt that it is true, and recollect now very realistically a dream that you used to have as a child. You may have forgotten it, but now you remember, and you will recall it most vividly now as I remind you of the details of that dream you used to have, of that dream you are going to have again.

At night, when you slept, as a small child, the same dream, recurring again and again, so that you were not sure that it was a dream, although it was not your usual waking reality either.

And beginning always in the same way, as, in the dream, you would get out of your bed, walking across the room to the closet, and finding that there is a door in the back of the closet. A door you could never find when you looked for it when you were awake, although often you did look for that door. But now the door opens for you in your dream, and you pass through the door to stand at the head of a stone staircase.

It is a very ancient-looking stone staircase, winding down and around, and in the dim light you begin going down the staircase, not at all afraid, but eager to go down, deeper and deeper, descending on down through the dream, going always deeper as you go down a step at a time, until finally reaching the bottom of the stairway to stand at the edge of what you recognize to be dark water, lapping, where a small boat is tied.

And now, lying on blankets in the bottom of the boat, the boat adrift and floating in the blackness, dark all around, but rocking gently from the motion of the water, back and forth and rising and falling, gently rocked as the boat drifts on and on, as the boat drifts down and down, as you feel only that gentle rocking, listening to the lapping of the water, nearing an opening where the boat moves along toward a light at the opening, and passes out of the opening and into a warm sunlight.

Still floating, downstream, feeling the warm sunlight, and a soft breeze that passes over you, as you drift down and down, and along the bank the birds are singing, and the fish are jumping in the water, and there is the smell of flowers and of the freshly cut grass in fields that have just been mowed. Feeling a great contentment, serenity, drifting drowsily down and down, down and down, with that gentle rocking, and now just let yourself feel it for a while. Be aware of this whole situation, the movements, the warmth, the sounds, the odors, as you keep on drifting down and down.

(Here the guide might pause to allow each player ample time to experience the images, and to allow for individual deepening, while the guide carefully observes each player to determine how fully a player may by now have become involved in the suggested image sequences. Then, in preparation for the mind game to be played, the guide might give these instructions):

Continuing now to float, to rock, gently, drifting deeper and deeper, until your boat approaches the shore and runs smoothly aground at the edge of a meadow. Leaving the boat now, and walking through the meadow, the grass against your legs, the breezes on your body, and conscious of rabbits in the tall grass, of the smell of the flowers all around, of birds singing in the trees, of the movements of your body as you walk, approaching a large tree and seating yourself beneath it, in its shade.

Sit there now, taking pleasure in all this, enjoying it just as completely as you can, and in a little while I will ask you to play with me that game we have come here to play, that game we made the long journey here to play.

But now, for a while, just feel your surroundings, be in a total harmony with all that exists here in this world out of time, this world without separations, this world where all is one, where you are one with all that is. . . .

*Effects of the instructions:*

Typically, with these instructions, and the expectations and intentions of the players, the guide will have enabled some of the players to experience with all of their senses the events and stimuli described.

Players who have responded fully will have experienced the journey about as they might if making it physically in the external world. In these cases, the player already has demonstrated a good capacity for achieving ASCs and for utilizing some of the potentials available in the altered state.

Other players may have made this journey as they might if observing a film that is effective in drawing the observer into its events as a kind of participant. Other players may have had a more or less rich fantasy experience, but without images (imaged sensations) of sight, touch, hearing, smell, or movement.

Some players may have experienced very little, and these persons should be encouraged, when the guide speaks, to imagine as richly as they can that they are responding so fully that they are full-fledged participants in the events described. This vivid imagining and making-believe will assist them in learning actually to make a full response and participation. These less responsive players also may be worked with individually, using various ASC induction procedures.

All players should know, and really understand, that new worlds may rise up around them to be experienced and lived in, and that their ways of experiencing the physical external world are also subject to countless modifications. Words are the means to the transformation of experience; but the capacity to have the experience belongs to the individual player, and the new worlds must rise up from within to fill, for a while, the player's consciousness.

*Durations of experiences, individual games:*

Some mind games by their very nature will require much more time to be played than some others. And in the case of a particular game, it will soon become obvious to guide and players that no hard and fast rules concerning duration can effectively be given.

The guide will continue with a game, or an induction, for so long as seems warranted in terms of the requirements of the group and of individual players. However, the requirements of an individual should not be met if this is detrimental to the other players.

The guide will learn timing by trial and error, by close observation, and by soliciting opinions.

As concerns duration, the guide will endeavor not to terminate any game prematurely. But the guide also will avoid so prolonging the games as to unduly fatigue the players. Very prolonged games must be avoided unless the guide is thoroughly experienced and the capacities of the players involved have been explored and understood.

*Trance and the reader:*

From this point on, in the "Mind Games," books, language and images will be used that, from time to time, will induce ASCs, or trance, in some of the more responsive readers.

A reader may recognize at the time that she or he is in an altered state of consciousness.

Or, that this has occurred, will be recognized later, when time "unaccountably" has passed, or when certain contents of the book are remarked to pass out of consciousness extremely quickly, as the contents of so many dreams do.

These trances, ASCs, and hypnoid states should prove relaxing and beneficial, and in some cases suggestions will speak directly to the unconscious, so that some of the benefits of playing the games may even accrue to some readers.

However, should a reader wish to terminate a trance state induced by the reading of the book, the reader will be able to do this by looking at the WAKE UP! image provided, looking at the image and, at the same time, clapping hands together loudly and also speaking, vigorously, the words WAKE UP!

This will take you back into your ordinary state, your cultural trance, or what is described sometimes as an "alert, normal waking consciousness." That is the state in which we all dream the same dream, more or less, and call it: reality.

Wake up!

For this first game of the first mind-games cycle, the players will seat themselves in a semicircle, and the guide will induce and deepen ASCs, utilizing the method previously described.

From the beginning players will be provided with evidences of their capacity to achieve novel and extraordinary states of awareness and that these are made possible by drawing on their own natural powers.

Even in the first mind games some of the players are likely to have extremely intense and possibly ecstatic experiences, and the magnitude of such responses will be instructive to all of the players, as examples of what is possible.

Guide (upon completion of induction):

In a moment I am going to play some music for you, some very sensuous music, but first you should know that it is possible for you to hear music very differently from any way you probably ever have heard it before.

It is possible, and this is what you will do, to hear music over the entire surface of your body, not hearing just with your ears. And over the entire surface of your body, know that there are countless end-organs that can be stimulated by the music, so that your entire body will hear, and that your body also is able to experience this music as touch sensations, music touching you everywhere.

Now, when I play this music for you, you are going to make use of this capacity of your skin to hear the music with your whole body, and to be touched by the music, all of your flesh caressed and excited by this music.

It will be an extremely pleasurable experience, the music swirling around you, passing in and out of your body, as your sensitivity increases, as you become more and more sensitive, more and more responsive to the music, until you are experiencing the music rapturously, exquisitely with all of your body, your flesh, your skin, all of you totally involved in this awareness of the music. And I will play it for you *Now!*

(The guide will have selected the music according to the composition of the particular group of players. During the playing, the guide may circulate among players, giving reinforcing suggestions, similar to those just described, if it seems that such reinforcement is required by some player or players.)

:: *2* ::

This second game may be played just after the players have completed their response to the music of the first game, and the guide then will say:

And now, I will play some more music for you, and this time *all* of your senses will participate in the music.

You will *see* the music, *taste* the music, *smell* the music, as well as hearing the music and being touched by the music.

A total and intense sensory involvement, as I am going to play for you now a different kind of music from that to which you have been responding up to now. And all of your senses will make individual responses, but, then, your senses will make an integrated, orchestrated response, each sense reinforcing every other sense, all of these responses coming together to create one powerful, climactic whole.

And I will play the music for you *Now!*

One person playing this game later gave the following description of just a few of the ways in which the music was experienced:

"At the beginning, it was as though this music was a molten, glowing, liquid substance; it was very cold, as though it was from my head down to the tip of my toes . . . and it was just filling all my veins. Then I just felt as though it became a part of my blood, as though I was just in a sea of this music . . . and everything else was just a sea of color, every color under the sun . . . color and rhythm, just ecstatic rhythm. A total sense of being united with this. . . . It had dimensions, round and full, a warmness and a coolness at the same time. . . .

"It was bright and yet it was quite inside. There was always a combination between being a very comic piece and being very exuberant and triumphant at the same time. But also tinges of sadness. And again, it felt sort of buoyant and tingly, but a feeling of being swept inside, like you just want to give yourself to it completely. It was absolutely pleasurable. . . . But it was felt inside and out. You felt like you were in the waves . . . at the same time, the waves in you."

After playing these games a few times, persons often are able to listen to music on almost any occasion with greater pleasure and awareness.

These games are among many exploring the possibilities for extending and intensifying pleasures, as well as for cutting short the duration and diminishing the intensity of perceived pain or unpleasure.

:: 3 ::

It is useful for players to learn early in the mind games something about how rich are the possibilities for experiencing one's own body and body image. This game, which we call an "Alice Game," with the ones preceding, demonstrates some of these possibilities.

At the outset, the guide induces ASCs by means of one of the induction procedures given in this book and in other "Mind Games" books. After ASCs have been induced and deepened, then the guide's words might be as follows:

Feel yourself to be extremely relaxed now, all of your body relaxing, relaxing more and more, and beginning to feel heavier. Your body becoming heavier and heavier, very, very heavy now, so heavy you couldn't possibly move it around, but not an unpleasant heaviness, just terribly heavy and, at the same time, totally relaxed.

And now that heaviness will begin to leave you, slowly at first, and then more quickly, as your body is becoming lighter, and lighter, until your normal weight has been reached, and then continuing to become even lighter, lighter and lighter, feeling light as a feather. And all of the weight going out of your body, until you are almost weightless, almost entirely weightless now, so that you could possibly float upon the air. And you may feel yourself to be rising just a little, levitating, floating just a little off the substance beneath you, and then settling gently back down once again.

Slowly, pleasurably now, discovering that your normal weight is returning, and it is very pleasant to become aware of your own flesh and the fullness of your body once again. And be very aware of your body now, and observe to your surprise that you are growing smaller.

Smaller and smaller, as Alice did when she drank from the bottle labeled DRINK ME, and you just keep growing smaller, down to four feet tall, and three feet, and down to two feet, and one foot, and growing even smaller, very, very tiny, right on down to about six inches, and you're now just six inches tall.

Feel that, explore it, how it is to be just six inches tall, and, like Alice, you might consider that if you get much smaller you could just disappear altogether, but you are not going to do that, at least not just now.

Because you are starting to grow in the opposite direction, getting bigger once again, on up to one foot, two feet, three feet, and four feet, and growing still more quickly, on up to your normal size, and past that, keeping right on growing and growing. On up to seven feet, and eight feet, and feeling at the same time a giant's strength, and energies, feeling very, very big and strong, and enjoying that feeling. And then, slowly, easily, returning to your normal size and normal body awarenesses once again.

But notice your body now as it becomes very dense, and your substance as it is changing, and you are feeling at first as if you are made of rock, and then of metal, and then of wood, and the wood becoming supple, feeling all of this quickly now, these changes in your body, your body very supple, like that of a young, energetic tree, full of sap, full of vital juices, able to bend and sway with the breezes, as you now do bend and sway with the breezes, all your leaves rustling, and the wind goes still.

And you perceive your body as more and more porous, so that the wind could just blow right through you, and now the wind is coming, a gentle breeze, and it does just pass right through you, a wonderful feeling of lightness, feeling of openness, of freedom, and now you *are* the wind.

Now you *are* a wafting breeze, blowing free, skimming freely along, rustling the leaves of the trees, stirring grasses, blowing in a gentle caress over plains and waters and bodies of animals and people, a hot wind passing over desert regions, a cool wind whispering to dreamers on an island.

And feel yourself now, as wind, slowly whirling, whirling, and becoming transformed into a human body, your own body, experienced as quite normal once again.

But remember, remember what you have experienced, and know that you can feel all these things, and that your body may feel itself to be of any size, of any shape, any substance, and that when you wish to, within the mind games context, you will be able to experience your body in just about any way at all.

:: *4* ::

At the completion of the third game, and without terminating ASCs, the guide will move directly into the fourth game, saying to the players:

Go deeper now, into this altered state, and continue going deeper, and deeper, as you are concentrated on my words, as you respond to what is said to you.

Remember what is said, and what is experienced in these games, and learn these things very well, your whole mind-body system absorbing, assimilating, and understanding.

And, as another phase of your instruction, we will take the first step in playing a game we will play more completely later on, a game that can become extremely profound and intense, extremely revealing, and a game that has been played by peoples throughout the world since the most remote times of which we have knowledge.

This is a metamorphosis game, a game that enables a person to become another life form, most usually an animal or some kind of supernatural entity, as it is played in rituals and magic all around the world. For the present you are going to get just a hint of what this experience can be, because it is important that you be well prepared by many mind-game experiences before you play this particular game too intensely.

And now you will feel that your body *is* changing, changing into the body of a cat, and you will feel a great contentment, and a sensuousness that is being satisfied as you feel yourself to be stroked and rubbed, and feel yourself very completely into that lithe, agile cat's body, feel the purring contentment, the sensuousness, the stretching, and enjoy all of this for a little while.

And now, easily, slowly, feel yourself ceasing to have the body of a cat, ceasing to be a cat, and returning back into your own body, as you become human once again, as you become yourself once again, your body, and your identity restored.

:: 5 ::

The guide will ask the players to be seated in a circle. (Or two persons might play this game, just sitting facing one another.) And the guide might say:

Relax now, everyone breathe deeply and rhythmically, inhaling and exhaling as you are directed, until your breathing is as one.

Good, and now remaining relaxed, meditate for a while upon this stone that is placed here before you. Fix your glance upon the stone, and keep your glance fixed upon the stone, until the stone breathes with you.

And the stone may change color, and its shape may alter, and you will witness these changes.

You will not wonder about the changes, but just quietly observe them, accepting their occurrence.

And now, identify with the stone, become the stone, and *be* the stone for a while.

Be yourself again.

Now the stone will be passed from one person to the next, and each of you will put pain into the stone, physical pain, and when each player has put pain into the stone, then the stone will be dropped into a bowl of water, and that pain will be washed away.

Each person again will put pain into the stone, now that the stone has been removed from the water and been dried. But this time, emotional pain, psychological pain, and then the stone will be dropped into the water, bathed, recovered, dried, and then passed around again.

Each player will put *pleasure* into the stone, and this time the stone will not be bathed, it will retain the pleasure.

The stone will pass from one person to the next again, and each person will put *desire* into the stone.

And the stone will be passed around the circle once again, and each player will put *love* into the stone.

Now observe, the stone is to be placed in the center, between the players once more.

Look at the stone, observe it closely, and meditate on the stone, fixing on it completely.

And now, once again, *become* the stone, experience the stone as you have helped it to be:

Purged of all pain and of all distress, and charged with pleasure, desire, and love,

and infused with something of the essence of each player, becoming a means by which each player knows more completely each other player,

becomes in some sense one with every other player.

Let go of the stone now, and return back into yourself, as the stone is to be covered with a cloth, so that you no longer will perceive the stone.

Blink your eyes,
stretch,
and now
*Awaken!*

*Gateways:*

It will be useful to use the word *trance* interchangeably with the term *altered state of consciousness,* and *trance* in these books should be considered a synonym for ASC, and without reference to any notions about hypnosis or about hypnotic trance that any players may have.

One very effective procedure for opening the doors to the experiential domain of the mind games uses this convenient term *trance,* and the procedure may be used equally well with individuals or with groups.

The guide might begin by saying to the players:

All right now, assume very comfortable positions and relax just as much as you can, making yourself very comfortable and relaxed as you find your awareness narrowing down to just what is being said to you and to your responses to what is being said.

And now close your eyes and attend to your breathing, as you breathe slowly and easily, and keeping count as you inhale and exhale ten times, and now do that.

And do it again, breathing and counting, but this time taking twenty breaths in and out, and becoming more and more relaxed with every breath you take, and with each number that you count.

Very good, and your eyes remaining closed now, imagine that you have with you here a notebook with pages and ruled lines across them, and that you also have a ball-point pen, and this pen makes very heavy, dark lines when you write. And taking this pen in your hand, and with the notebook open, at the left-hand side of the page you will write your first name, or whatever you call yourself, and over to the right of that, and on the same line, you will write just the word *trance.*

Next, back over to the left, underneath the place where you've first written your name, you will now write your name again. And, over to the right of that, just below where the word *trance* first appears, you will write the word *trance* again.

And over at the left, writing your name, and over to the right, writing *trance*. On the left, name, on the right, *trance*. Writing your name, and then writing *trance*, and the name, and *trance*, and the name, and *trance*, and continuing to do that for a while, and just doing it over and over again, as you do go into trance.

You will *feel* that you are going into trance, and when you feel that you *are* in trance, then you will stop writing for just a minute. But until you feel that, and you really know it, you'll just keep on writing your name, and *trance*, and name, and *trance*, as many times on as many pages as you feel that you should write it.

But now, however far you may feel that you have gone with this particular procedure, you will stop and then start writing again, but this time over at the left, under the last place where you wrote your name, you will now write the word *deeper*. And just over to the right of that, just under where you wrote the word *trance*, you again write the word *deeper*.

Over at the left, writing *deeper*, and over to the right, writing *deeper*, and continuing to write, *deeper* and *deeper*. And as you write *deeper* on the left and *deeper* on the right, the trance will deepen, and you will go deeper and deeper into that trance, and feel yourself going deeper and deeper.

The writing will carry you deeper and deeper, and you will just be aware of the writing and of the voice that is speaking to you and of going deeper and deeper into trance as you continue writing.

After a while you may feel that you have gone just as deeply into trance as you can go at this time, and when you feel that you are just as deep as you can go, then you will put the pen down and you will close the notebook. And you will just sit there waiting, as if in a kind of bubble outside of space and time, a kind of comfortable little eternity that you will wait in, very restfully, for a little while.

During the course of the foregoing instructions to the players, the guide will carefully observe each player and especially any motions that a player may make with his hands. Some players will go through the physical motions of writing and of stopping, so that the guide will know by observing those players that they have achieved an altered state and are able to respond very well to the suggestions being given. Other players may not go through the motions of writing, but it still may be evident to the observer that the player is responding. With still other players, the guide may be uncertain as to the degree of response, but in any case the guide should now proceed as if there were no question but that all players are responding to a considerable extent and so will be able to carry out additional suggestions as these are given. Then the guide will begin the game for which this entry exercise has prepared the players.

At the end of a mind-games session, the guide will terminate ASCs or trances, effecting re-entry back into the ordinary state of consciousness of the player, the everyday waking state, and the guide might accomplish this by saying:

This session now is about to end, and in just a minute or two you will be led back into a state of alert, waking consciousness.

I am going to count from 20 up to 1, and as I count you are going to find yourself becoming wider and wider awake, until at the count of one you will find yourself opening your eyes, and you will be wide awake, and refreshed, and pleased with what we have accomplished here today.

Every count will bring you closer to the surface, as I count now: 20, 19, 18, 17, 16, 15, and you will be aware of energy entering your body as I speak to you. Right up through the soles of your feet, a tingling, and energy coming up into you through the soles of your feet. A very good feeling, so that when you do wake up you will be both rested, and refreshed, energized, and very alert, a good, happy feeling.

And 14, 13, 12, 11, 10, and you are half-way back, and 9, and 8, and 7, and 6, and 5, and you are three-quarters back, feeling very alive and refreshed now, and moving up toward an alert, waking state, and feeling better and better, as I count 4, and 3, and 2, all of that energy coursing through you, as you want to stretch and move around in your body, feeling how alive you are in your body, as I count 1, and you open your eyes, *wide awake*, as I clap my hands loudly now, *wide, wide awake!*

Wake up!

## :: 6 ::

After ASC induction and deepening, the guide will advise the players that they are going to play a game that may tell them something about current attitudes a player has toward the player's own body and parts of the body, and it will be of interest to try to determine what the unconscious mind is thinking about the body, or, perhaps, what the body is thinking about itself.

The players should be cautioned that the images and symbols which will emerge as this mind game is played, quite likely do not reveal very much about any absolute values or understandings that the unconscious mind may have. If the same game should be played tomorrow, or next week, very different images and symbols might emerge. So the players should understand that what happens during the game are just examples of transient attitudes disclosed during creative expressions by the unconscious, or by the body of the player.

And the guide then will urge the players to go deeper, and to listen as the guide will mention various parts of the body on which the player's attention is to focus. And as the player directs awareness to that body part, an image will arise into consciousness, visual and seen, or just verbal and known, but an image that is symbolic and expresses something about the body part.

The players will remember these symbolic images and afterward will construct a kind of map or diagram of the body, utilizing the images that emerged as the mind game was played.

First, the guide might ask the players to focus attention on the feet, and to await emergence of an image in some sense symbolic of what the feet mean to the player. Then, the hands, obtaining a symbol for the hands. And after that, perhaps, the abdominal region, the guide allowing in each case sufficient time for the symbols to emerge and to be appreciated by the consciousness of the player.

Next, the guide might call attention to the chest, and the shoulders, to the neck, to the face, to the back, to the genital region, and finally to the top of the head, and the brain, reminding the players from time to time that later a body map or diagram is to be created.

In some cases, the images will come up very quickly, and fully formed, while in other cases it may be that the symbol will undergo a process of development and change before settling into any final form, or it also may be that the symbol consists of a sequence of images, all equally important, so that there is no single final form.

For example, the images, seen with the eyes closed, by one player, included the following:

Abdomen—swirling, cyclone shape; colors changing quickly, a great deal of energy.

Feet and legs—like tree trunks, but not rooted, it's funny.

Shoulders—two mountain peaks.

Pelvic area—a butterfly, with wings, head, antennae, soft wings that are moving.

Head, above the eyes—I am looking at the interior of a very large blossom, many petals, a lotus I think, and I am looking up from inside at the petals. There are veins of light, white, creamy light, an inner luster, so much light along the veins. The inside of the petals changes, there are flowing colors, green, creamy, throwing off light, and now just the colors remain, the form is gone.

Entire body—shafts of light, bright in the middle to light colors at the edge, kind of a rainbow with fine bands of light making up the whole. The bands are so fine it is hard to distinguish them and you could mistake it for a solid light.

This player was asked if she understood the symbols, and at once responded that she did understand them clearly, or so it presently seemed to her. Her interpretations then included the following:

Abdomen—combination of sexual energy and assertiveness.

Pelvis—femininity.

Feet and legs—desire for contact with the earth, these are the vital contact points.

Head—the beginnings of spiritual growth, but there remains much to learn.

Entire body—points up the need to integrate everything.

When working with a group, the guide may want to tell the players that they will understand the meanings of the symbols as they emerge, and recall these meanings later, to be recorded along with or as part of the symbolic body map.

But then the guide should also caution the players that interpretations made in this way are as susceptible to error as interpretations made in any other ways.

:: 7 ::

For this seventh mind game, as for the fifth, the guide will not formally induce altered states of consciousness or trances.

However, as the game is being played, it is quite likely that many of the players will develop ASCs of varying depths and the guide should be aware of this possibility, making careful observations, and behaving accordingly.

At the end of this game, as at the end of all mind games, the guide will carry out a re-entry and awakening exercise for the players, and the guide will do this just as if there had been a formal ASC induction.

To play this seventh game, the players will be seated in a circle or semicircle facing a large plant, a potted plant that can be removed. For example, the plant might be a fern.

The guide will ask the players to breathe rhythmically together, breathing deeply, in and out, ten or twenty times, or however many times seems desirable. Then the players will chant OM together for several minutes, all the while looking at the plant, and intending that the image of the plant will sink in very deeply, be very thoroughly remembered, so that it will be practically impossible for anyone to forget that plant soon.

The image of the plant will be recorded exactly, after such prolonged and extremely close viewing, and the awareness of the players should be narrowed to consist just of the rhythmic breathing and of looking at the plant.

Then, for two minutes, exclusive, intense awareness of the plant, and nothing else, just a total awareness of the plant.

The guide then will advise the players that the plant is going to be taken away, but each player should continue to look intently at the place where the plant was, and imagine that the plant is still there, and affirm a belief that the plant *is* still there, meditating on that plant that really *is* there.

The guide will return the plant to the place where it was before and then will remark to the players that the plant is more or less conscious, that they should consider the very certain fact that the plant is more or less conscious, and as they look at the plant to let this really sink in, to be aware of the plant as a conscious, living being.

From the most ancient times people have believed that there are certain plants, such as the mandrake, which scream when you pull them from the ground, and the guide will remind the players of that.

And he will tell them that there was an Indian scientist at the turn of this century who seemed to have recorded with his instruments that a tree will scream should someone strike it with an ax or otherwise injure it, and that other experiments have been done with plants and trees subjected to positive and negative statements and that trees that have been cursed in some of these experiments have died soon afterward.

Moreover, every player should know that presently experiments are being done with contemporary scientific instruments that appear to indicate that if some living creature is killed or injured in the same room or in an adjoining room nearby where a plant is standing, that plant will show an awareness of what is happening to the injured organism, and will even suffer a little of the pain being undergone by the other life form.

And this suggests that there really may be an underlying unity of all kinds of life, a pool of consciousness in which every being is affected by whatever may happen to any other being, so that even plants partake of the pool of consciousness and are able in some sense and to some degree to share the conscious experience of all other living things.

Players should now close their eyes and breathe deeply, relaxing and breathing deeply and easily, as they begin to listen to the plant, trying to feel what the plant may be feeling, trying to tune in on the consciousness of the plant.

And now, just for the duration of this experiment, players will believe that there is a kind of indwelling spirit of the plant, which they may be able to communicate with, and one player might address to the plant a question about whether the plant has anything of value that it wants to impart, anything that could be taught.

The plant's answer might be experienced in terms of frequencies, vibrations, muscular responses in the person, feelings, visual images, or whatever. The thing to do is to be open to this communication, to receive whatever is communicated by whatever pathways the communication might arrive.

After this, the players will be told to open their eyes and to look closely at the plant again, to meditate visually on the plant and to observe any changes that may appear to be taking place in the plant, whether of color, or form, or whatever, and to take note of any ways in which the plant is being seen differently from ways it has been seen before.

Then the player should consider the whole experience of the plant, identify with the plant, *be* the plant for a while, and feel what it is like to be the plant, experiencing the being of the plant, and knowing what it is, really knowing.

Finally, the guide will suggest to the players that each return to a full normal awareness of her or his own body, each identity completely restored, and after the arousal-re-entry exercise, it may be of interest to discuss the experiences individual players have just had.

:: *8* ::

The guide may say to the players:

I want you to know, and understand, that you have the capacity to remember past occurrences *completely*, remembering with such detail and vividness that it can be as if you are reliving an experience, and so far as you are concerned you really are living through that experience.

The total revivification of experience is the exercise of memory at its very most powerful. But it also is possible to remember with great vividness while not being quite so caught up in what is happening that the recalled experience is indistinguishable from a present reality.

As you learn to use your mind more effectively, you will become able to remember more, and to remember much more vividly, even becoming able to revivify past experiences if you want to do that. And do fully understand that this is not just your old way of remembering, just a feeble kind of knowing what happened, but a memory that recaptures all of your sensations and feelings, so that the past does rise up with an extreme richness for you.

Now, on this occasion, we will begin to explore that potential you have for remembering those parts of your past that you decide you would like to remember, or that it is specified you will remember.

We will explore that, as you close your eyes now, listening attentively to me, just the words that are spoken to you, and you may feel that you are going into trance, and going deeper, or you may require a little longer to go into trance, but you will do that, and go deeper and deeper, going deeper, and you won't think about that movement down, and in, but just listen, and respond to what is being said to you.

Letting the words just ripple over you, swirl around you, around and around you, drawn back into the past, or down, into the past. And is past down? Or back? Or is there any place that is past, or any direction leading to past? Or present? Present is no place if past is no place, but present moving back and down into past, or past moving into present, and which is past, and which is present, and what is present is past, and past is present, as you go deeper now, and just keep on going deeper, as the words keep swirling, round and round, and round, about you, and over you, leading you deeper, deeper down.

Going deeper, and going back in time, the past becoming

very accessible to you, so that you might even find yourself in a present that you thought was past. But now it is here, and you are in the midst of it, and you can remember exceedingly well, if that is the way we want to put it, because you can go back now in time, and you *are* going back.

Back one year, and two, and three years, and knowing how old you were about three years ago. And, when you were that age, you had an experience that made a very strong impression on you, and you will remember that experience very vividly as you move into it, finding yourself in the midst of that experience, and it is happening to you *now*, and you *are* living that experience.

. . . Going back further and further now in time, back and back, and your body is changing, becoming younger, and becoming smaller, as you move back in time to about your tenth year of life, or ninth, somewhere around that time, when something happened that you would like to experience, something important, or exceptionally pleasurable, or giving rise to a good deal of happiness, so that you do want to experience it, and it will come vividly into your awareness.

Feel yourself in that body you have now, that small body, how that body feels, its strength, its weaknesses, how its senses function, and becoming aware of the setting, the people involved, the relationships, all about that experience that comes so vividly into your consciousness now. And you will have plenty of time to go through this experience, and do go fully into it *now*.

. . . Aware of my voice now, and going even further, further back into time, becoming younger, moving in your child's body, knowing childish emotions, childish ideas, imaginings, knowing how you are relating to other persons, to the world around you, and going back, and back, to the oldest, earliest, extremely happy and pleasurable experience you can arrive at, letting it come up into consciousness, and letting that experience happen to you, as you touch, and smell, and listen, as you look, and taste, and move around, and there is plenty of time for you to have this happen to you, and happen very fully, very richly *now*.

. . . Now, once more, trying to go back, or just finding that you are going back, to an even more remote time, and finding the earliest possible experience that you now can become conscious of, even an infantile experience, with the feeling of being a tiny baby, if you can go that far. In any case, a feeling of being very small, very, very young, and knowing something that made you awfully happy, that gave you great, great pleasure, and experiencing that for a little while, but long enough, and really experiencing that most completely.

Good, and now it will happen to you that you will move forward in time as I speak to you, returning to the age you were at the beginning of this game, and the age you are as I am speaking, gradually moving back into present time. And bringing back with you all of those happy and pleasant experiences, remembering them in detail, and remembering them not just as verbalized memories, but remembering with your whole body, and bringing all of that happiness and pleasure along with you, back with you, as you move now into the present time.

The guide will give players instructions for waking, and then there will be a discussion of the experiences the players have had.

## :: 9 ::

The guide will instruct the players to pair off, and each couple is to be seated with the players facing one another.

And the guide will say:

This game can be variously described as an exercise in role-taking, in being someone else, in experiencing someone else who is being you, and in exploring how consciousness may become altered in the course of these approaches to interpersonal relationship.

You don't have to understand those words, but you will come to understand by doing. Just as you don't have to know who you are, or who your partner is, to play this game, and in fact you don't know, do you? But you can look very closely now at your partner, while you are listening just to me.

You will look at each other, and keep looking, but also letting your muscles relax, and breathing deeply, conscious of relaxing, and of breathing deeply, and easily, and keep doing these things until your total reality consists of relaxation, breathing, and feeling consciousness altering, consciousness deepening, as you look ever so closely, without wavering, at your partner, and attend to what is being said to you, and that will be the whole of your reality, as you go deeper and deeper now, and keep going deeper and deeper.

Now, as you keep looking at the face in front of you, you will notice changes in that face, maybe subtle changes at first, but then more drastic changes, so that sometimes you will note that the face you are looking at now is not the same face you were looking at a moment before, and now just look at that face for a while, observing the occurrence of those changes.

You may have seen many changes, or a few, and while you were observing those alterations, you were being looked at by your partner, and you were undergoing metamorphoses for your partner, and you don't know how you looked, how many faces, how many different identities you assumed for your partner as you were being observed.

But you do know now that each person has many possibilities, many appearances, identities which may be waiting to emerge, and the possibility, too, of just being a screen upon which appearances, possibilities, and identities, may be projected by someone else. And the face that you customarily wear, and the way you are ordinarily seen, has nothing necessary about it, so that in some other time or place you might present a quite different appearance, or be seen quite differently by other persons, even if you observe no difference in your appearance as compared to what you think that appearance is in your everyday life at the present time and place.

Going deeper, and feeling yourself going deeper, and listening, and beginning to consider what it would be like to be that person you are confronting. Going deeper, and wondering what it would be like to be in that body that sits there facing you, and beginning to know, to feel yourself into that mind-body system sitting there, and feeling yourself slipping into it, as identities transfer themselves between bodies. Going deeper, and into that body, so that it *is* you.

And now, feeling that you really are being shaped in your thoughts and your feelings by your body, so that your new body increasingly gives to you the identity of that person who a while back was other, touch whatever you are seated on, knowing how *this* body touches things, and let the fingers feel, and the palms of the hands, remarking these new sensations, and remembering.

Taking on now all *this* body's perceptions, looking out at the world through *these* eyes, and looking over there at that person opposite you who *was* yourself, and from *this* new perspective seeing that person who used to be yourself, and getting up and moving around, experiencing the consciousness that goes with the movements of *this* body in which you now are, and looking at the movements of *that* other body playing *this* game with you.

Together with your partner now, examine the sensory possibilities, drinking water for example, passing an object back and forth between you, walking along holding hands and remarking what that hand that was your hand feels like when touched with the hand of this body in which you now are, and which is you.

Being that awareness, being this person, how do you feel about the world around you? Are you any less happy, or wiser, or are you less wise, and are you more or less fearful than you were before, more or less angry, more or less loving? And are you more or less alive, feeling everything very keenly, fully, knowing it as this person in this body, as you have become, and as you now are?

And now, slowly, find yourself moving back into the body that normally is yours, your consciousness shifting back into that body, and this transference is easy, fast, complete, as you are now that person, that body, as you were before this game began, although retaining anything of value you have learned.

Fully yourself now, although quite possibly still feeling that you are in an altered state of consciousness, a trance, begin to discuss with your partner the experiences you had while playing the game. And try to determine how valid were some of the experiences you had, how complete the identification may have been, and whether you believe that these are valuable ways or not of learning something about another person, and possibly of increasing mutual understanding, or otherwise improving interpersonal harmonies and communications.

Later, the players as a group will also probably want to discuss these experiences, and it might also interest the players to make experiments in which not just one but several players assume the identity of another player, then comparing experiences to see how similar were their thoughts and perceptions while identified with that person.

At the end of this game, the guide will, as always, give suggestions to achieve an alert, energized, refreshed, waking state.

The foregoing confrontation game with observation of altered perceptions of the partner also can be played by couples or groups divided into couples as a "reincarnation game," with the understanding that the phenomena observed are not really evidence pro or con for reincarnation.

For the duration of the game, however, players will accept a belief-system to the effect that the faces observed reveal to the observer some past life and appearance of the partner.

The observer will record the faces observed—nationality, age, sex, all facts noted—and later one player will describe what was seen to the other player, then saying, "Try to recall that life for me."

Then the other player will await what comes to mind, and let the question be answered in this way, without any conscious effort to invent or otherwise create an answer.

:: 10 ::

The group will be guided in shared breathing and then in shared chanting exercises.

The guide will produce a canvas or large piece of cardboard suitable for drawing, along with other materials to be used by the group in creating, by a collaborative effort, a work of art.

The guide might explain:

This work of art we are going to create during this session is a first symbolic expression of the collective consciousness of all the players.

In the future, we will create other works of art, and this will be a valuable measure of how the group consciousness may be altering.

Alternately worked on by each player, when completed the work we are going to create will serve as an important object of meditation for us.

Looking at this work, created by all of us, individual egos will become porous. Individual minds will cease to be separate. The islands of isolated individuality will begin to move together, overlapping as we continue to establish a single mass-collective consciousness—one mind, by means of which the group will begin to live as an entity apart from the individual existences of the particular players.

Upon the completion of this initial expression the players will talk about it, reaching some agreement about what is being expressed.

Neither will this mind game end there.

During the interval between this meeting and the next, there will be a flowing together of the minds of all players, happening especially during a portion of your sleeping and dreaming life.

During that meeting of minds in the altered states of consciousness that are dreaming and nondreaming sleep, members of the group will begin to work to advance and strengthen the collective consciousness first embodied and made material in the work of art we will now create.

We will create that work, and as we do, as we work on it, you will experience yourself as going into an altered state, and the deepening of that state, and already that begins to happen, as one by one I touch you, indicating the order in which you will go to create our work of art.

Going up to the canvas to create it, and at first doing something that will not seem to be anything more than a very private expression of your own state of awareness and that of the group as you believe it to be. But gradually, as you return to the canvas, acquiring a sense of what the group actually is expressing in this work of art, so that with increasing understanding and unity of purpose that work of art will finally be brought to completion. And it will be a work that is expressive of all of us, and of the one purpose we all are.

:: *11* ::

The guide will open the session by inquiring about dreams the players may have had since the last meeting that may be relevant to the forming of a group consciousness.

Then the guide will advise the players that the present session is for the purpose of creating a kind of entity that is an expression of the collective consciousness of all the players and that will be called by them the Group Spirit.

This entity may come to be in some sense independent of any individual player, although it has been created and is sustained by the players.

As the Group Spirit is brought into being, the players will understand that they are creating a larger and more complex awareness than they would have access to just by pooling the knowledge and talents of individual members of the group.

The Group Spirit will be more than just a summation, and it will be to some extent autonomous, but at the same time the Group Spirit must be understood as nothing more than a symbolic form, a purely mental construct, having the sole purpose of serving the needs of the players.

The guide will next lead the group in prolonged, rhythmic breathing exercises, instructing the players to pay careful attention to the breathing of everyone present, working together until all the players are exhaling and inhaling rhythmically together as one unit and one breathing.

Following this the guide will lead the group in chanting of the OM for some minutes.

Next the guide will instruct the players to be increasingly and intensely aware of a growing unity and oneness, of the group as it is growing together, of how this is nourishing the Group Spirit. That the players should be able to unite in a collective consciousness, and that the players should be able to create the entity, Group Spirit, out of the collective pool of consciousness, should be understood by everyone as extremely important.

What is being done will seem strange and alien to some players (especially those not familiar with practices of a similar nature long known in the Far East), but everyone will come to understand what is being done and how it is important and valuable, and this will become clear to each player as the games progress.

And now each player will relax as completely as possible, and continue to relax, letting go, and relaxing completely, but listening with total attention to what is being said, and when told to do so echoing silently the words of the guide, repeating silently the words of the guide when instructed to do so, and responding powerfully to those words and to the repetition of them.

The guide saying:

> Repeating now after me,
> We are becoming one,
> becoming one.
> One mind, one mind, one mind.
> One mind, one mind, one mind.
> One trance, one trance, one trance.
> One trance, one trance, one trance.
> One ever-deepening trance.
> One ever-deepening trance.
> Becoming one.
> Becoming one.
> One mind.
> One mind.
> One trance.
> One trance.
> One ever-deepening trance.

And now, that trance continuing to deepen, we all will believe, without reservation, and for the duration of this game, that by flowing together we really can create this entity, the Group Spirit, and communicate with it, ask it questions, and that this Group Spirit we have made to be will have access to information and perceptions inaccessible to us by any other means.

The guide will then choose from among the players one player who will serve as oracle, prime communicator with the Group Spirit. This will be a person, if one is available, who has demonstrated a capacity for achieving very deep trances, profoundly altered states of consciousness, and who is well able to move about and function in every way while remaining in deep trance.

This person will interrogate the Group Spirit in behalf of the group, will receive the answers and sometimes interpret the answers, and will have the important task of obtaining from the Group Spirit instructions about how the players can best proceed to do what is most productive for them, most creative, most evocative of their capacities, helping players individually and collectively to realize in the fullest measure their potentials.

By means of this entity, the Group Spirit, and with the help of this person, the oracle, there can be an effective tapping of the great riches of the collective unconscious brought into consciousness. Knowledge and solutions can be attained to that could not be attained by other means.

The players will, on a number of occasions, call forth this Group Spirit, and it will grow stronger as they learn to more effectively give it life and strength. For now, all of the players should experience an outflowing into a pool of consciousness apart from any person, and become aware of the stirrings and rising up out of that pool of the entity being called Group Spirit.

If the entity is sufficiently strong, interrogations may begin. If not, it may be decided to wait until the next occasion to enter into dialogue with the entity.

In either case, and when appropriate, the guide will instruct the players to feel themselves becoming detached from the pool of consciousness, flowing back out of it, fully regaining her own identity, his own identity, the ego fully restored, individuality fully restored.

But better able, with each exercise, to let go of the ego for a while, much more easily able to create a oneness and, out of the oneness, to energize the Group Spirit.

The guide will then instruct the players that very soon the session will be terminated, and that there should be a leisurely and comfortable re-entry, an unhurried return to an alert, refreshed waking state.

There will be a count from one hundred up to one, and with each count the player should become more and more aware of energy flowing into the body, feel more healthy, feel more vigorous, more and more alive and alert in every respect while moving toward wakefulness.

And, moving up to the count of one, a normal state resumed in every way, but wider awake, more energetic, than when this mind game began.

:: *12* ::

After ASC induction and deepening, the guide will advise the players that they are going to explore some important aspects of time-space orientation and how this orientation may affect various sensory perceptions, and also mood and thought processes.

The guide will inform the players that shortly they will hear a metronome beating, and this metronome will *always* tick at the rate of exactly sixty beats a minute, and it should always be known and experienced that the metronome is beating at the rate of precisely sixty beats a minute, and under no circumstances will there be a deviation from this rate, so that if a player supposes that there is any change in the rate, that supposition is an error.

The guide will then activate the metronome, which is beating at sixty beats a minute, and then will slowly speed up the metronome, the change at first being very gradual, while the players again are told that they will experience the metronome as beating at the rate of one beat each second, sixty beats a minute. But the guide will increase the beats to seventy, and eighty, and ninety beats a minute. Then the metronome will be slowed, back down to sixty beats a minute, and on down to fifty, and forty, and thirty, and twenty beats a minute, the guide every now and then reaffirming that the metronome's rate is precisely and undeviatingly sixty beats a minute.

The guide will conduct this experiment at a leisurely pace and will observe the players carefully in case that it later might be of value to interrogate closely certain players who appeared to be making strong responses. Then the guide will ask the players to remain just as they are, except for two changes in the situation, and only two, that each player should open her eyes, or his eyes, and that each player should listen to the metronome, as it beats at exactly sixty beats a minute, and know that she or he is now, once again perfectly oriented in time.

At this point, the players will be asked to describe anything unusual that was experienced during the exercises just ended, and there will be a discussion of any phenomena of interest.

These reports, if typical, will include the information that when the metronome was speeded slightly, players variously felt euphoric, active, excited, and, when the speed was greatly increased, felt somewhat manic, overstimulated, possibly a little anxious.

When the metronome was slowed down slightly, players variously felt lazy, relaxed, possibly a little drowsy, and if the beating was slowed down more, felt lethargic, and then drained of energy, tired, possibly a little depressed and anxious.

Still greater alterations in either direction will produce more drastic and unpleasant changes in mood and thought and sometimes in various sensory modalities also. Then, if the metronome is beating rapidly, players will greatly welcome a slowing, and if the metronome is beating very slowly, will greatly welcome an increase in the rate of beating.

The guide will demonstrate again that the players can respond to changes in the metronome's rate, and the players will be asked later to reflect on the meaning of what they have experienced, and to know that these reactions become more powerful as the trance states are deeper, and to think about what this might mean.

Next the guide continues:

And now, the eyes closing again, go deeper, be aware only of what is being said, and when, on request, the eyes open again, it will be perceived that colors are more vivid, forms more distinct, and that there will be a very marked increase of depth perception.

The players will be asked to keep going deeper, and still deeper, and without changing anything else, to let the eyes open.

Typically, this will result not only in the perception of a rich, beautiful world around, but in very positive emotion, and in occasional cases of something akin to a religious type of experience.

Players having enjoyed these perceptions for a while, the guide will request that eyes be again closed, and that all perceptions be normalized, and the guide then might say:

I am going to count from twenty to one, and as I count you will feel the energy coursing through your body, and you will feel extremely alive in your body, and when I count to one, you will be wide awake and you will move around very alive and vital in your body, refreshed, just feeling awfully good, and I'll start counting *now!*

:: 13 ::

After induction and deepening, the guide will remark that mind games may be utilized to cleanse the doors of perception, to restore the capacity for experiencing with something like the full potentials of the various senses. Most persons have blunted or diluted sense perceptions, and one reason for this is just that through familiarity and habit they have ceased to really look at, or touch, or otherwise take in the world around them, except in a most impoverished way.

Then the guide will say to the players:

But now imagine and believe without any reservations that every experience you are going to have here and now is a novel experience, something new to you, something you have never known or done before.

The guide might then present to each player successively a container of water. The player, eyes closed, putting fingers in the water, as the guide says:

I offer you contact with something entirely unknown to you, something to be touched and known by you for the very first time.

And the guide will repeat this, giving to each subject a piece of fruit, a sponge, a stone, some bark—whatever the guide has brought along to use in this exercise.

Then each player will be given bread to eat, and instructed:

Taste now, something that you have never tasted before, and slowly savor it, really coming to know it, everything there is to know about it, and about yourself in relation to it.

All right, and now let yourself become completely relaxed, be comfortable and relaxed, and find yourself going deeper and deeper, deeper and deeper into this altered state, continuing to go deeper as you slowly open your eyes and look down at one of your hands.

Look at that hand as if it is just a thing lying there, and it is not your hand, just *a* hand.

No longer anything but just a hand, a thing, and it might as well be a piece of wood, or a stone, just a curious-looking object, and it feels nothing so far as you can tell.

And now, I would like you to reach out and touch it, stroke it, move your fingers through its spaces, feel its texture, and know this curious object resting there before you with the tactile knowledge given to you by your sensing hand.

And now look very closely at that lifeless, detached hand lying there in front of you, and as you look at it, you will feel a sense of connection to that hand, faint at first, and then becoming stronger, as you feel the life beginning to flow into it, feel the animation, a returning sense that this hand is part of your body, is connected to you, is you, and move the fingers a little, and begin to touch with it.

Touch your leg, touch whatever object is closest to you, and now feel that hand becoming more and more sensitive, more and more sensitized, better and better able to touch and to know.

That hand will become still more sensitive, still more sensitized, until the sensations experienced by and through that hand are just extraordinarily acute, exquisite. And now touch your other hand with it and you will notice that this hand is now far more sensitive, much better able to know and to experience, than that other normal hand that previously touched the desensitized hand, when it seemed to be detached and lifeless, an unaware thing.

Now, look at that hand again, that sensitized hand, and feel your consciousness flowing into it. Put more and more of your consciousness and your mentality into that hand so that it will seem to you that that hand has such awareness that it almost can see and hear and listen to my voice, and now that hand *will* feel my voice, as if the hand has end-organs for hearing, and now you will find yourself hearing with your hand.

And now you will find that hand becoming very, very sensuous, sensual, so that whatever it touches, you will find an extremely pleasurable sensation occurring, even a voluptuous kind of sensation, very much like an erotic sensation, intense. And textures will just rise up to be stroked by that hand, caressed, and you will find yourself having now such pleasurable experiences with that hand, those fingers, that you'll know you never remotely knew before how sensitive those fingers and that hand could be, how much they could touch, how

44

much knowledge and pleasure they could give you if you would let it happen, and if you knew how to go about letting it happen.

Look around you now and see if there is someone you would like to share touching with, and who wants to share that with you. And, if you have a partner, place the palms of your hands together, those deliciously sensitized hands, and let the two hands know one another, and see how much of that other person comes through those hands in which the consciousness has now been localized and intensified.

Touch fingertips for a while, and then bring the fingers together, locking the hands, but not tightly, together, and feel now the consciousness and the energies moving from one hand to another, circulating through the hands, and then let those hands slowly, very slowly, draw apart and separate.

The whole body is learning, the players are learning, how sensitive it is possible for a hand or any other part of the body to become once one has broken through the old habits, the old conceptual modes, once we have begun to think and behave in new ways that allow us to cleanse the doors of perception and to regain something of our complete sensory acuity, regaining capacities our bodies still have and are able to exercise once we break through to freedom and know without obstruction the rich world of stimuli around us.

The guide then will instruct the players that all parts of the body will be experienced as they were before the game began, but that the players will have learned and will remember. And with practice they will be able to regain the sharpness of perception that was experienced during the game.

The players then will be counted back to an alert, waking state.

## :: *14* ::

This is a game individuals may play alone, between sessions of the group. The guide will describe and assign it, probably at the close of the thirteenth session. The guide will instruct the players that the principal benefit of this game comes from the playing of it, the accustoming of the player to unusual phenomena experienced in solitude, and not from anything that is likely to be learned in response to specific questions posed during meditation.

The player, naked or clothed, will seat herself (or himself) before a large mirror, using a candle or the flickering reflection of a fire to induce or help induce the altered state of consciousness.

She sits looking at her own image in the mirror, breathing rhythmically for a while, relaxing completely, anticipating that a trance state will come about, and concentrates upon the image as an object of her meditation, seeing not as if it were her own body, but just as if it were an object being meditated on with the aim of inducing a trance or altered state.

The player will focus upon this image, and expect to perceive as she watches a colored aura around the edges of the image, and she will look at the image until colors flow all around the edges of that reflected image of her body, and she will note what those colors are.

Next, she will look intently at the image, instructing herself, Now, go deeper and deeper, deeper and deeper, and finally she will ask aloud the question: "Who have I been?" And she will breathe deeply and rhythmically, repeating silently the question: Who have I been? And as she meditates on the reflected image, she will notice changes in the face and whole body.

There may be changes in age and race and sex and in the color of the hair, the color of the eyes, the height and weight of the person, all sorts of changes may take place as she repeats, over and over, the question: "Who have I been?" "Who have I been?"

Should she note some especially remarkable change, or should some change arrest her attention, then she will endeavor to maintain that image and address it, and ask as many questions of it as possible concerning the life that the particular appearance may have had.

After performing this meditation, with its question: "Who have I been?"—she will stop asking this question and will meditate upon her reflected image with the intention of looking at it until it seems to her not to be her own image at all. The aim of this meditation will be to sever the connection between the person and the reflected image, until all sense of identity with that image has been lost.

When that exercise has been concluded, the player will again fixate on her image, instructing herself to go deeper and deeper, while concentrating intently on that image, and she now will ask the question aloud: "Who am I?" and continue meditating on the image, repeating silently the question: "Who am I?" "Who am I?" "Who am I?"

And she will observe changes occurring in the image, as she keeps on repeating the question, and later she will record these changes she observed and will reflect upon them, and after that the group may discuss the changes that she and other players observed.

In addition, the results may be used by her as a basis for still other mind games, and, for example, she may successfully suggest to herself that she will have dreams in which those persons or appearances figure as characters, and in those dreams there will be a considerable elaboration, so that she will have much more information concerning the image that appeared to her, or the image that her unconscious mind projected.

And, finally, the player will look closely at her image in the mirror and she will ask aloud the questions: "Who will I be?" "Who will I be?" observing the changes in the image that occur.

Then: "Who will I be next year?"

"Who will I be a decade from now?"

"Who will I be a hundred years from now, or a thousand years from now, if I am to be at some more or less remote future time?" And she will be observing the changes that occur.

"Who will I be at any time at all in the future, if I am going to be again, after this present life has been concluded? Who will I ever be?" and observing the images, and remembering, and later recording.

After that: "I am looking at *my* image now, my image as it

is here and now, as it normally and rightfully is, and this *is* my image, this is the reflection of my own body as it now is.

"And I will now terminate this mind game, doing it by counting from twenty up to one, feeling, as I count, refreshment, energy, a great deal of strength, all pouring into my body, into my body which at the count of one will be very fully alert, and feeling very good about things, totally alert and refreshed when I reach one, as a termination of this mind game I have been playing.

"And I will begin counting *now!*"

## :: 15 ::

A variation of this game may be played by two persons, confronting one another, each meditating on the face of the other, and observing changes which occur.

As, for example, one player asks aloud: Who am I? Who am I? and the second player keeps looking intently at the first player until some change occurs, to be taken as suggested by the question.

Then the second player will ask aloud: Who am I? Who am I? and the first player will await and observe the visual transformation as it occurs.

And the players may continue with this until each has asked all of the questions meditated on in the preceding game, both players taking active and passive roles, either alternating roles for each question, or one player asking all the questions first, and then the second player asking all the questions.

At the end of the game, each player will restore the partner to a refreshed, alert, and energetic state, also declaring that with this the game has ended.

## :: 16 ::

The guide will welcome the players and inform them that this will be the first occasion for the experiencing by some of the players of the Rite of Liberation. Several of the players will be selected to participate in this rite, which will be performed on other, subsequent occasions, until it has been experienced by each one of the players.

Players selected as initiates in the ritual each will stand confronting two other players, one of these players being male and the other female.

The guide will announce that an extremely important ritual is to be performed on this occasion, and that only those players who are completely willing to participate in something very powerful but potentially most beneficial should be initiates, and that anyone who feels inadequately prepared, too anxious, or otherwise unready to proceed, should now withdraw and await initiation at some future time. Those who feel themselves ready will be seated, and at the side of each initiate will stand the male and female player assisting that initiate in the ritual.

The guide will now engage in a prolonged induction of an altered state of consciousness, and deepening, until by the guide's estimate each of the initiates has reached the most profound depth achievable by those players at the time.

The guide will then speak, and the male and female assistants in the rite will behave according to the words the guide speaks.

And the guide will say:

We gather here now in this place for the purpose of performing a timeless ritual to free your mind-body, to free you, in all aspects of your being, from limitations imposed upon you willfully or by ignorance or accident, by your fellow human beings.

We, representing all those powers that crippled you, now act to restore your powers and your freedom to you.

Assuming all responsibility for what is being restored to you, for removing all the fetters that bind you, we lift the burdens and chains of the past from you, even as we do fully accept you, and whatever you have done and been.

We take your hands and we restore to you the full capacity to know and to take pleasure in the sensations of touch, and in all other sensations of your body.

We touch your eyes, so restoring your vision, that you may see clearly and delight in a freshness of vision.

We touch your lips, and you are free to speak.

We touch your chest, and you are free to breathe.

We embrace you, and you are free to respond to embraces and to express yourself sexually.

We touch your forehead, and you are free to think, to know, and to realize the fullness of your possibilities.

We, representing your father and your mother, and your sister and your brother, your friend, your lover, representing all of humanity, do now set you free.

Loving you, we free you to love and to be loved.

We accept you, honor you, recognize you as at once uniquely yourself, and as a harmonious part of the great whole.

We honor you, as you know awareness of your liberation.

In the name of humankind, and of all Being, we welcome you to freedom.

It *is* done!


The guide then announces that there will be a period of silence during which the initiates will experience a serene but extremely powerful emotion, and during this time all that has been said will be accepted and learned and understood and imprinted upon the total person, the whole mind-body of the initiate.

It will be integrated, and it will always be a part of that person, from this time on, and always.

After this period of silence, the duration of which will be determined by the guide, on the basis of observation of the players, the guide will slowly, gently restore the initiates to a refreshed wakefulness.

:: *17* ::

The guide will instruct the players that with this game the conclusion of the first of the four cycles of the mind games has been reached.

An exercise now will be performed that may be very valuable to each player in letting the player know something significant about the current state of his being-in-the-world, about his unconscious, about who he is, and who and what he thinks he is, at the present moment in time.

This same game will be played again, at later stages of other mind-games cycles, and the emerging symbols will be compared from time to time as a measure of change in the person, as a possible measure of personality growth, spiritual and other development the player is undergoing and achieving.

Players will be instructed to relax, breathing exercises will be carried out, and one of the procedures followed for the induction and deepening of altered states of consciousness.

Each player now will be instructed to conceive of herself or himself as being represented by a series of concentric circles.

How many of these circles within circles there are will vary with the individual player. Each player will work with the number of circles appearing as a visual or other mental image, and the player will know that the outer, larger circle represents the surface, the more superficial aspects of the person.

And each of the circles within the outer circle represents some deeper and progressively deepening aspect of the self, until the innermost circle, the center, will represent the essential person, the self in at once its deepest and most comprehensive reality, as this may be knowable to the player at this time.

Each player will be instructed to meditate on the outer circle until there comes to mind, as visual image or other mental image, a symbol representing the self in its outer, more superficial manifestations.

Players will next meditate on the circle just inside the first one, achieving a symbol representative of the self on somewhat deeper levels, and this meditation will be repeated until the player arrives finally at the innermost circle.

Players will be told that when they are ready to meditate on this innermost circle, then that person's head will involuntarily and slowly fall forward, and she or he will wait, and while waiting will be aware of nothing, think of nothing, just being there and awaiting the further instructions to be given by the guide.

When, in the opinion of the guide, all players have reached this waiting state who can do so, then the guide will instruct the players to meditate upon the inner circle, by this means effecting the emergence of a symbol that will represent the self at once most profoundly and most comprehensively.

Then, this symbol should be meditated on, and the player should observe most carefully every aspect of the symbol and be able to remember it, and be able to bring it back into consciousness when the altered state is terminated.

If possible, then, the player should draw or paint the symbol, but, in any case, should clearly remember it, because it will provide a basis not just for discerning future growth, but also for the playing of some other mind games.

Each player will be urged to feel this symbol deeply, feel it and know it with the entire body, understand that this may be a vehicle of growth and self-actualization, and that by arriving at the symbol a process has been initiated, a profound dynamism of the self has been activated.

And now, within each mind-games player, something has been unleashed that can bring strength and health and joy and self-realization, and each player should remember this while returning slowly, easily, at the player's own pace back to what is called by us the normal waking consciousness.

And each player should bring back peace, serenity, something of the energies and the harmony of the depths of the self that have been touched and that have been made conscious.

At the conclusion of this game, the guide will congratulate the players on having completed the first cycle of the games, and will advise them that they now are ready to proceed to a second, deeper, more mysterious, more profound exploration of our own inner space, of ourself, and of the world we live in, as we discover who we are and what we have to do.

*Mind Games:* **BOOK TWO**

# A Special Note to Mind-Games Players:

It is not possible to read with understanding Book Two of the mind games without having first read Book One.

It is not possible, and should not be attempted, to *play* effectively the Book Two mind games without first having played, in order, the games given in Book One.

This order of reading, and even more of playing, is *necessary* and no leaping over is possible, no short-cutting is possible, without inevitable and considerable loss.

Mind Games Two is a new cycle, enabling the players to go beyond, deeper and beyond the experiences and awarenesses of Mind Games One.

Mind Games Three will go deeper, deeper and beyond Mind Games Two.

And Mind Games Three will be just a prelude and a preparation for the final cycle, called Mind Games Four.

The games were created to effect a progression, a spiraling and deepening, a planned and tested expansion that is aimed at leading the players at last into ways of knowing and being not open to the players before.

*Preliminary meeting:*

On the occasion of beginning this second cycle of the games, the players will hold a preliminary gathering, to choose the first of the guides who will enable the players to move more readily along the continuum of consciousness and to other spaces, exploring and achieving.

After the completion of this selection, the guide will lead the players in relaxation and breathing and chanting, as this practice has become established in the group.

The guide will then perform the ASC induction, by means of a procedure taught in "Mind Games: Book One." This is the writing, with imaginary notebook and pen, of the name of the player, and then of the word "trance," enabling players to go deeper and deeper, deeper and deeper, until the guide feels that altered states of consciousness that are as profound as possible at that time have been achieved.

Each player then will be instructed to remember:

Remember completely, remember *everything*, about this state you are experiencing now.

Learn it, learn all about what it is, so that you will find it again, quickly and easily, when you want to do that.

And now, if in the past you have experienced any state of consciousness you consider deeper than this, recall it, and keep going deeper and deeper, until you have reached that depth. And then, just keep going deeper still.

And on each one of the occasions when we meet, you will be able, very easily, and very quickly, to regain this state, and even go beyond it, learning on *every* occasion to *go deeper, always* learning to *go deeper and deeper, and doing it* when that is desirable for the most effective performance of the particular mind game we then want to play.

*Trance and the reader:*

As she or he continues to read in this book, it is very likely that the reader may become aware that a trance state has occurred at some point during the reading, so that the reader also has the opportunity to learn about altered states of consciousness in a direct way, and many readers will do that, will *go into trance*, and learn, and benefit from that learning, and possibly from some of the mind games as well.

This trance, resulting from reading the mind games, probably will be experienced as a pleasant state of rather profound relaxation, and with a high degree of immersion in the materials being read, so that afterward it may seem that the time spent reading passed very, very rapidly, and there also may be difficulty remembering what has been read, keeping what has been read in memory, in the way that so many dreams are difficult to remember, to keep in mind for very long after the dream has ended.

For the reader in trance, it will be possible, if the reader has no objections, to respond to the instructions to *go deeper*, and that deepening will be experienced, will be felt as it happens, so that the reader will know what a trance is, and what it is to *go deeper* into a trance, and will do it, experience it, because that is a valuable learning, and also may be a very pleasurable experience.

And the reader always will know that he or she can easily terminate the trance induced by reading this book, and be able to do that by looking at the WAKE UP! image and, at the same time, clapping hands loudly together, and speaking, vigorously, the words WAKE UP!

Wake up!

The guide might begin by saying to the players:

Please make yourself extremely comfortable, as comfortable as you can, and after you have done that, then just practice relaxation for a while.

Relax, relax a bit at a time, and do that until you feel yourself to be just as relaxed as you can get.

And now, please listen closely, very closely, all of your attention focused on what is being said to you.

You know what an altered state of consciousness is, you know what a trance is, and we are using that word *trance* to indicate an altered state of consciousness, and you do know what a trance is, and I wish that you would think about what a trance is.

Remembering what a trance is, and remembering so well that you are re-experiencing what a trance is, going into trance, and feeling it, knowing it, as you go into trance, what a trance state is, and how it gets deeper, and *going deeper* when that comes to mind.

Going deeper and deeper, and as you do that, you are learning to go deeper still, and you will go even deeper, and you will do that in the time you have at your disposal, and you really will go deeper, you really will, and you will do it *now*!

Listen again please, and remember now just what it is like to dream, that state you are in when you are sleeping and when you are dreaming, and in just a little while you are going to re-enter that state, and you will dream.

Listening, and responding, and having no awareness apart from that, no reality apart from that, and finding yourself as you listen becoming drowsier and drowsier, as I speak to you, and you respond, becoming sleepier and sleepier, approaching closer and closer to that state in which you are able to dream.

Getting still sleepier, as I keep talking, and it doesn't matter much what I say, whatever it is you will keep getting sleepier, but you will also remember what was said.

And now, before you do begin to dream, I want to mention to you that from this time on, you will begin to keep a dream diary, writing down all you can remember of your dreams, and as you keep doing this you are going to discover that you can recall your dreams better and better, in more and more detail, so that your dream diary will consistently become more detailed and more accurate, and these recorded dreams are going to contribute to your development, your self-understanding, and the keeping of the diary will also be important to your successful playing of future mind games.

Going deeper, getting sleepier, and feeling more and more as you do when you are in your dreaming sleep. Sleeping, sleeping, and going faster asleep, faster asleep, and in a little while now you will have a dream. You will have a dream, and it will start when I tell you, shortly, to begin. But you should also know that after a while I am going to tell you to stop, and when a voice tells you to stop the dream, then everything is just going to freeze, the dream images just will freeze at that moment when you are told to stop. But now, as you sleep ever more deeply, you will begin to dream, and you will dream, beginning right *now*!

The guide will allow a few minutes, or longer, if that appears to be desirable, for the players to respond to the suggestion that they will have a dream, and then he will instruct the players to *stop*, and he will speak to them further:

Now, remaining in this state, this state in which you are able to dream, watch as the images of that dream you just were having become very clear, and then slowly dim out and fade away. But you will remember the dream, and you will record it in the journal you keep to describe your mind-games experiences, but not in the diary you keep for recording your nocturnal dreams, because those nocturnal dreams have to be recorded separately, and they have their own book, a book that is just for those dreams.

And now, sleep deeply, deeply sleeping, and you are going to have another dream, and this dream will be a recollection, a re-experiencing of a dream that you had a very long time ago, a dream you may have forgotten all about, but a dream that was important to you at the time you had it, and you will have that dream again, and you will have that dream beginning right *now*.

When time has been allowed for the dream, and with the responses of the players well observed, then the guide might say:

Very good, and you will remember that dream, and at the end of this session record it, writing it down just after you finish writing down the dream that you had just before this one.

And you will please listen carefully now, because I am going to give you a strong suggestion, a very strong suggestion, and what I am suggesting to you is that tonight, when you go to bed and have fallen asleep, deeply asleep, you will have a dream and that dream will be about the dream that you just had here.

Understand clearly, tonight you will dream, and that dream will be a dream about the one you had here just a moment ago, and tonight's dream will be an interpretation, a clarification of the recollected dream that you just had here.

And tonight, as soon as you have had that dream, you will wake up, and be wide awake, and you will be very strongly motivated to write your clarifying dream down as the first entry in the dream diary that you're going to keep and keep very faithfully.

Then you will go back to sleep, and later, in the morning, you will examine what you have written and see how that dream interprets and clarifies the dream you had so long ago and that you re-experienced here today, just a little while ago.

Sleep deeply now, a deep, refreshing sleep, from which you can awaken as from a good, uninterrupted, all-night-long sleep, although you now will sleep just a few minutes of time as measured by the clock, but it will be enough for you to have that very good, deep, refreshing sleep, and after that I will speak to you again, but have that sleep beginning *now*.

After several minutes, the guide will ask the players to listen and respond to what will be said to them, and then the players will be given suggestions for arousal to an alert and refreshed waking state.

:: **2** ::

The guide will induce and deepen ASCs, and then will lead the players through sequences designed to develop further the capacity to experience richly subjective realities, and to stimulate imagination by the eliciting of vivid images evocative of the creative process.

The guide could say to the players, for example:

And now you find yourself going deeper, your closed eyelids heavy but relaxed, as it grows darker and there is a sense that you are drifting down, and down, until you find yourself standing at what you perceive in the gloom to be the entrance of a cavern.

Standing there, and then going inside, moving down into the cavern, and when you round the first bend in the cavern you will find that it is lighted by torches in holders thrust into crevices in the rocky walls.

Flickering lights, and shadows, and as you continue, down, and down, you are *completely* alone there, and going deeper, becoming aware of a dampness in the cavern, and now hearing water dripping as if from little springs somewhere off out of view.

You can reach out and touch a fungus that is growing on the walls, and on the big rocks that are scattered along the way you are going, and far off, in some other part of the cavern, you can hear the fluttering of wings, as if bats had been disturbed, so that they fly around and collide with one another for a little while, and then resettle.

Moving down and down and down, deeper and deeper, and as you go deeper down in this place, you find that the trance state is deepening also, and you know that it is deepening, and going deeper, until you come to a pool, a small circular pool with very clear water, and it is light enough here for you to lean over the edge and see your image reflected clearly in the pool.

Look into that pool, look closely, and keep looking for a while at the image of your face reflected there, an image almost completely unmoving now, just very faintly stirring with the slightest movement of the water.

But now I am going to put my hand down into the water and stir the water in that pool, and as I do that stirring, the water will swirl around and around the reflected image, and then the image will be drawn into that swirling.

And the image will appear to you as if it were at the center of a whirlpool, a whirlpool that is drawing the image down and down and down. You will feel your consciousness in that image, and that it is your body there, it is you and you are being drawn down in the swirl, being drawn down and around and around and down, swirling and circling deeper and deeper and deeper, and then just feeling yourself sinking, drifting, sinking, down, down, through waters that are very comfortable to be in.

There is no problem here about breathing, and you don't even have to think about that, but just being aware of drifting down and down and down, and going deeper and deeper, and finding yourself to be out of the water, in a circular place that is dry, and you will notice that you are standing on a stone floor and at the very bottom of an immensely deep, cylindrical, carved-out space, far, far below the surface of the earth.

And now, if you look around you, you will discover that the walls are all made of heavy, gray rock, and there is no opening to be seen anywhere, except that if you lean your head back and you look way up, you can catch just a glimpse of the opening, far overhead, through which the light somehow reaches down down to that deep, deep place where you are.

And you'll become aware, and you'll see, that I am standing here with you in this circular room or place, and we are standing inside of what seems to be a kind of magic circle, and you will observe that there are many curious symbols inscribed around the edges of this circle. You don't know what those symbols mean, but you know and are confident that they are very, very powerful, and that you will be perfectly secure so long as you remain with me inside of this circle.

Here, in this very deep place with me, and I want you to look in the direction in which my arm is pointing, and I am going to make a sweeping gesture with my arm, and as I do that, you will see that a segment of the wall will open. And in that opening, you will see a world that you have long since forgotten, or only barely remember.

It is a world that belongs to another time, a time within your life that is distant, when you were a very small child. And as you look at it, you will see it as a world that you remember fondly and nostalgically, and you will appreciate it with the senses and the mind of the child you were at the time when you were a dweller in that world. You will experience that childish world, and experience that world as a child again, and you are going to do that now for a while, until I speak to you again.

And now, be fully aware that you are here in this magic circle with me, and I am going to make another sweeping gesture with my arm, and the wall will close, and again we are alone, surrounded by this massive wall of rock, while encircling us, at our feet, are those mysterious and extremely potent symbols carved into the stone.

I am going to move my arm yet again, sweeping it across a space a little distant from where the earlier opening was, and you see that the wall is opening, and there is a ledge, and on the ledge is a large crystal ball.

You are able to see clearly inside of the crystal, and you will see that a tiny fetus is floating there in that crystal, and it is alive. It is human, and living, and as you watch, the fetus will develop, and it will grow, and as you keep watching it you will have plenty of time to see it complete its whole cycle of fetal development, and then be born.

You will observe this baby being born, and watch it grow, becoming one year old, and two, and four, and five years old, and living through more of its life, and being ten. You will watch the whole life unfolding before you.

And just observe with a keen interest that human life developing and unfolding before your eyes, and watch until you have seen to what age that being will mature, how old that being is going to become as you watch, and you will have plenty of time to observe this.

It will all seem to happen at quite a normal pace, although as time is measured by the clock in the world of your everyday existence, it won't take much time at all for all of this to happen. But just intensely observe now, and be aware of nothing else than the development of that life.

The guide will allow about four or five minutes, unless observation of the players indicates that a little more or less time is needed, and then will say:

You are going to remember exactly what you have seen and otherwise experienced. And you are going to know that in this kind of world you are able to visit, that within these subjective realities, all kinds of things can happen which would seem to be completely magical if they happened in the external world, with your ordinary reality and consciousness.

Understand that in these other spaces we go into while we are playing the mind games, you are free of various of the limitations which ordinarily bind you. You have access to powers, awarenesses, experiential capacities ordinarily blocked, but you will learn to bring many of these capacities productively to bear in the external world of the consensual reality which has to be maintained, but which can and must be expanded.

The guide will then awaken the players and request accounts of what happened when the player was instructed to observe the crystal and the life form growing within it. And it very often will be discovered that each player has seen in the crystal the birth that is later recognized to have been his or her own birth. And as the player observes the child growing up, it will become evident who the child is, and there will typically be no disguise by symbolism or failure to recognize the identity or understand what has been seen.

In some cases, however, the player will view her or his own life, but it will be symbolically veiled. In such cases, unless the guide is very experienced, it will be best not to attempt to explore this symbolism or suggest to the player that the symbols may refer to the player's own life.

The more typical kind of experience was briefly summed up by one player as follows:

"The fetus must have been me, though I didn't know that it was me until much later. The crystal was a mirror facing a mirror, so that you could see everything thousands of times. Each image was like a progressing step, so that I knew I wasn't really seeing every minute of the life, yet nothing important seemed to be omitted. When, inside the crystal, I had reached my present age, a bolt of lightning shattered the crystal, all of those thousands of mirrored images, and I was looking at myself, at the happiest moment I will ever have. I was wearing a kind of ocher-colored robe. Happiness emanated from me, my whole body was glowing with happiness and warmth."

:: 3 ::

An all-night session of the group will be held, preferably in an out-of-doors setting that is pleasant and private.

The principal purpose of this session will be to experiment with ways of inducing and deepening altered states of consciousness, enabling players to learn to go very quickly and easily into altered states and, most important, to achieve a greater depth of trance.

The chosen guides and players already able to achieve deep trances, will work intensively with other players.

Group inductions may utilize fire as a focal point for concentration, and prolonged listening to the beating of drums, dancing, chanting, and whatever other procedures the guides may have decided on in their earlier planning for the session.

Players will be encouraged to practice self-induction of ASCs, and for several hours it may be desirable to go through numerous inductions, superimposing one ASC on another, without any terminations, to alter consciousness more and more profoundly.

Guides, on this occasion, will also experiment with induction procedures of their own devising, and will observe which procedures are the most successful, then calling these to the attention of the other guides.

Each player, including guides, will be given one ASC induction during which the player will be told:

And now, not just your mind will be in trance, but your whole body too, and you will soon become aware that it is happening: to your hands, and you feel it, and your feet, and moving in from your extremities, until your entire body is in trance, your entire mind-body in trance, and going deeper, and deeper.

After this particular induction, which can be developed in much greater detail, the guide, when waking the players, will remember to include the instruction that "the mind-body will waken when the count reaches one"—not just "*you* will waken," as might ordinarily be done.

:: *4* ::

The players from time to time will participate in a type of mind game we call "Visionary Anthropology": the exploration and study of imaginal worlds.

These games help to familiarize the players with aspects of the creative process as it always has been experienced by persons of genius and high-level creativity, in the arts, but also in many other fields.

The guide will induce and deepen ASCs, and then might say to the players:

Now you will observe a rounding of your body, that you are feeling yourself to be circular, feeling yourself in the form of a ball, a sphere, and now you *are* quite round.

You will notice next that the sphere is moving, and in fact that you now are hurtling at a very great rate of speed across vast reaches of space, traveling, on and on and on and on, until you find yourself gradually slowing down, and coming to a stop.

Your body is resuming its normal shape and feeling, and it is feeling normal now, and you are looking all around you to discover in what place you might be. But it is strange, it is a new world that you are in, a reality you have never known before, and it really is strange, and new, so that it will be very interesting for you to explore it.

And you *will* investigate this world, its flora, its fauna, all of the animate and inanimate forms that are a part of this world. If there are humanlike beings or any other intelligent beings with whom you can communicate, you will meet them, and communicate very fully with them, finding out everything that you can about their culture.

If they have a music, you could bring back one or more songs from that world. If they have an art, you may return and be able to reproduce some of that art for us well enough so that we all will have some notion of what it looks like.

You may want to make some inquiries about laws, customs, philosophies, religions—whatever is of interest and that you are able to learn.

This is just the first of various trips you are going to make as an anthropologist, and explorer, visiting other worlds and dimensions and experiencing those realities in very rich detail.

And now you will have some minutes of earth clock-time to carry out your studies, and that is all the clock time you will need, because in the world where you now are, you might have days or weeks or months or even years of experience before I tell you that it is time to come back to this world from which you started out on your travels. And now, just start off in any direction that appears to be promising to you, and begin this exploration.

After five minutes or so, in part depending on observation of the players, the guide will give instructions that the players will find themselves returning to the space-time from which they started, and then there will be the usual restoration to an alert, refreshed waking state, and after that there may be a discussion of what has been experienced.

Players who might feel that they did not finish what they had to do in the imaginal world, may be told that it usually is possible to return to the same world again and again, exploring it just as fully as one might want to explore it. And players who have described unusually rich worlds, may be encouraged by the guide to go back repeatedly to bring back from that world treasures which might enrich our own with works of art, songs, stories, scientific knowledge, mathematical discoveries, inventions—whatever is worth bringing back and can be brought back.

:: 5 ::

Many variations on the visionary anthropology mind games are possible.

The players, after ASC induction and deepening, may be directed to find themselves in a time tunnel, a tunnel of swirling energies bearing them back and back through time, to a place and time designated by the guide, or the player may be told to make a choice, or the player may be told that he will just spontaneously stop when the time and the place are the right one.

This going back through time can be made into a reincarnation game as well, the player being told that she will go back beyond her own present life to a time and a place where it will seem to her that a past life was lived. And she will then live that life for a while, experiencing the personality she was in that past life, and also gathering information about the world in which she once lived.

For all of these games, the guide may wish to program the

players to believe in the reality of what they will experience, and this should be done after ASCs have been induced, but before the instructions concerning the playing of the game have been given. Then, the players will be told to believe, for the duration of the mind game, in the reality of their experiences—for example, that the past life was really lived—and to believe this completely, without any questioning of the experience, and to believe this until, and just until, the game has been ended with the termination of the trance.

## :: 6 ::

The guide will induce and deepen ASCs, and then may address the players as follows:

Please give me your complete attention now, being aware *just* of what I am saying, and I want to remind you that many of the best scientific minds of our time agree that in the vast-nesses of the universe many other intelligent life forms must have evolved. They hold it to be completely reasonable to suppose that intelligent life exists in many places throughout the universe at this present time.

Now, this intelligent life might exist on other planets, but that life might also exist in space. It might exist in dimensions which overlap our own space-time, and it is very likely that such alien, intelligent life forms do exist, and in some ways and places we have not even thought about.

Moreover, it is also quite possible that some of these life forms have developed along lines similar or close to our own. Or, if they are very dissimilar, that their intelligence is so great that they can communicate with us, understanding what we have to tell them, and enabling us to understand what it is that they would like to communicate to us.

And they might communicate in our language, or they might communicate by means of images seen by you, or images heard by you, or you might just know without hear-ing, or seeing, or using any of your other senses in any way familiar to you, what that message is.

I want you to understand, too, that the very best way and

perhaps for the present the only way, is within the context of an altered state of consciousness. And this may be true for the reason that within that range of states we think of as normal, conscious contact with these other life forms has been made impossible by some kind of shielding against it, an involuntary, shielding function we carry out without even knowing that we are doing it. By altering consciousness we sometimes drop the shield, and the contacts then become possible.

Go deeper now, deeper and deeper, and now in this altered state you will firmly believe and know for the duration of this game that it *is* possible for *you* to make such a contact and you will be able to specify to some extent what kind of contact it is that you would like to make.

You will intend and open yourself to contact with some being of an intelligence greater than human, but not so much greater that no communication is possible. And as you become open to communication, you will send out powerful feelings of love and good will, being fully receptive, but accepting and welcoming only those entities whose feelings toward human beings are benevolent ones, who will not harm you intentionally or unintentionally, who will return the love and good will you are offering, and who truly wish to communicate something to you.

And you will find yourself now becoming very passive and receptive, very open, drawing in the intelligence, the entity that will respond to this openness, to these feelings.

Several minutes of earth clock-time will be enough to allow you to have a fully and seemingly quite prolonged experience of whatever being comes to you. And you may wish to obtain instructions from that being about how contact may be established again on future occasions, so that repeated meetings might take place.

After four or five minutes, unless observation indicates more time is needed, the guide will say to the players:

Be aware now that the time available for this communication is exhausted, and any entity you may have contacted understands that you must end the relationship for now. It is ending, and you find yourself gently separating from that contact, slowly withdrawing, and it is understood that there can be no further communication by you with these alien life forms until such time as we intentionally create conditions for the contact.

The guide will then restore the players to wakefulness and experiences will be described and discussed. Should it happen that some player has had an unusually important experience, then the guide will induce and deepen trance and that player will seek to re-establish the contact, the other players being observers. If the contact is made, then the guide and players may be able to participate by questioning the intelligent being manifesting to the player in trance.

As in all games with programed-in belief systems, the procedure to terminate ASCs will include a reminder that the programed system was for the duration of the mind game only and will not affect the player once the game has ended.

*Accelerated mental process (AMP):*

In altered states of consciousness it is possible to make use of a phenomenon that has been called "time distortion," and that we have preferred to call "accelerated mental process," or "AMP."

It long has been known that in dreams and trances, psychedelic drug states, and other altered states of consciousness it is possible for the mind's activities to become so accelerated that an enormous amount of subjective experience can occur within a very brief period of clock-measured time.

A man falling from a bridge, and expecting to die, but who by some chance is saved from that death, may later recount that during the fall his whole lifetime flashed before his eyes, or that he then relived his whole lifetime, or at least relived all significant events, so that it seemed that his whole lifetime was lived through, and lived through without any haste, events all seeming to happen at the same rate as they happen during everyday waking experience.

Persons who have taken psychedelic drugs sometimes feel that hours have passed, or days, or even much, much longer periods, only to discover that all of that mental experience occurred within just a minute or two of time as measured by the clock.

And it is this very greatly increased rate of functioning on the subjective experiential level, that is meant by acceleration of mental process, or AMP.

In the induced ASC, or trance, this AMP phenomenon may be controlled very well, so that, for example, it becomes possible to instruct a mind-games player who has seen a particular film—let us say a very long one, such as *Gone With the Wind*—that she will have just two minutes of clock time, but those two minutes will be quite enough for her to have the experience of walking up to the ticket window of the same theater where she saw *Gone With the Wind* sometime past, and of buying her ticket, walking into the theater, taking a seat, and seeing the whole movie through again, from beginning to end, and then getting up and strolling out of the theater, all of this seeming to happen at just a normal pace, and she will have had all of this experience in just two minutes of clock-measured time, *but with suggested AMP.*

This distinction between subjective or experiential time on one hand, and objective or clock-measured time on the other, should be well understood by the guide, and well explained by the guide to the players, and it should be discussed by everyone until it is certain that the concept has been grasped by all members of the group.

It then will be very productive to utilize AMP in many of the mind games that remain in this second cycle, and in the third and fourth cycles of the games.

Guides and others will thoroughly familiarize themselves with AMP or "time distortion," and its many important applications, by reading the volume by Cooper and Erickson recommended in the "Guide's Book for Mind Games," and also the authors' own *New Ways of Being*, upon publication.

The guide will induce and deepen ASCs, and then will advise the players that they are going to make an application of their capacity for accelerated mental process, or AMP. At the same time, this mind game will explore another phenomenon of great interest: musical images in the creative process.

This is the music produced by the unconscious, experienced as auditory images, and many great composers have been able to somehow open themselves up repeatedly to this music from the unconscious, and some of their compositions have been little more than a writing down of what was heard.

These composers include Brahms, Wagner, and E. T. A. Hoffmann, along with many others, and Hoffmann used to say that he never consciously composed music at all, if by that was meant some effortful process of creation. Instead, he would say, "I just sit down, close my eyes, and play what I hear."

And the guide might say to the players:

You now understand what AMP is, and you understand about musical images, and now you are going to have the experience of hearing a musical creation as those composers heard their compositions.

When I tell you to begin, you will have two minutes of clock time, with AMP, and you will have an experience under the conditions I will describe to you, but not beginning until I tell you it is time to begin.

Go deeper now, and listen only, be aware only of what is being said, and in just a little while now you will find yourself walking down a street paved with stones, and soon you will come to a very pleasant-looking, small café, and you will want to go inside, and you will do that. You will go inside and sit down and order a sandwich and a bottle of beer, or whatever you might want to drink, although the beer is awfully good, about the best beer you will ever taste.

After you have had a little time to enjoy your drink and your sandwich, you will look up and observe that on the stage the musicians are about to play, and there may also be a singer, or perhaps not. Then they will play a song, or several songs, and these will all be songs that you have never heard before anywhere, songs being heard for the first time here in your own interior theater.

But it will be experienced as a quite real theater, and you will listen closely to those songs, and try to learn them so you will remember them later. You will stay in that place just as long as you want to, and then you will come back out into the street, and stroll along until I speak to you again. And at some future time you might want to sing for the rest of the players one or more of the songs you will hear, the songs you are just about to hear, as you find yourself on that street, approaching that café, beginning *now!*

A similar game may be played in which the player is told that he or she will experience, in a minute, or two, or three, a short work of fiction, a kind of vignette, hearing it or perhaps experiencing it visually as well, or even with all of the senses, and then remembering so as to be able to describe it orally later, or write it down.

## :: 8 ::

This mind game may be played either with or without suggested AMP and preset clock-time limits. It might be played both ways, and results compared. Or, better, a similar game might be devised, and one played with and one without a suggestion of accelerated mental process, and the results then compared and discussed by the players.

The guide will accomplish the induction and deepening and then might say to the players:

Now you are about to have an experience that will involve you in many sensory, emotional, and symbolic changes, and reorientations in time and space as you experience the internal rhythms and cycles of nature on the planet earth, knowing it all as it happens spontaneously to and with your mind-body system.

Your mind-body, when I tell you to begin, is going to experience the seasons as they are happening within you, so that you will feel the coming and passing of the seasons as an objective occurrence, but also in the deeper and mythic meanings of this progression. These meanings will be personal for you, but they will also be larger than that, and universal.

Go deeper now, and be completely attentive, and when you are told to begin you will experience, first of all, the springtime, new life growing and coming to be. And then the summer, the heat and the ripening, the sultry sensuousness of the summer.

And then the fall, the autumn, the richness, the lightness after the heavy heat of summer, the crispness, the differences in vitality and growth. And after that, the winter, the maturity, the knowing, the ending, the cold and the dying, knowing your own dying.

And after that, finally, once again spring.

And, with the spring, rebirth, joyous ecstasy, hope in the sense that all life is renewing, feelings of youth and a sense of surging, certainty that life continues, freshness recurring, feeling it keenly in your body, and exhilaration of highest intensity. You will know all of this, and more, and you will know it fully.

In just a moment I will tell you to begin, and you will have about five minutes of clock time, experientially all of the time you could possibly need to experience most completely what you have been told that you will experience, experiencing it in your unique way, as your own self, your own person contributes the details.

Now you will begin, starting with the spring, and beginning *now*!

At the end of this five minutes, the guide may ask the players to remain in the present altered state of consciousness, but to open the eyes and take a look around, and also to touch objects in the immediate environment. Then the players will be asked to close their eyes, and the trances will be terminated.

:: 9 ::

With a frequency depending on the needs of the group, mind-games sessions should be held which have the principal objective of enabling players to achieve deeper and deeper trances or ASCs.

Through practice, most players should learn very quickly and easily to experience altered states, to induce and deepen these states in themselves, as well as being able to respond to the suggestions of a guide.

Having learned to self-induce and self-deepen the trances, players will practice utilizing these ASCs and the capacities available in altered states. Possible utilizations will be learned by players as they play the games. Applications should be made in terms of wishes and problems of the individual—anything from self-entertainment and problem-solving to self-regulation of pain or pleasure responses, or any of countless other possibilities that will come to mind.

Once a player has learned to respond to induction by the guide, it usually will be possible to give the player a word that can be used by the player to quickly self-induce trance.

The guide, having deepened and induced the altered state, might say to a player:

Now, in just a moment, you are going to experience an image that can be described with just one word, and that image is going to be one that will have the greatest effectiveness for you as a means of inducing an altered state of consciousness. So that, if you should want to self-induce ASC, then you will just pronounce the word, once, or it might take a few times, and your eyes will close and then you will *see* the image, or be very strongly aware of just what it looks like, should it happen that you do not see it. And now, your eyes becoming very heavy, your eyes closed tightly but without any strain, go deeper, and deeper, and in just a moment that image will appear to you, and when you have that image you will tell me what it is.

Or the guide might assign a word to a player, although it more often will be most effective if the player finds her or his own image and word, as the unconscious offers this image into consciousness.

And the player might find, or the guide might assign, the image-word "butterfly." Then the guide will waken the player and work with the player repeatedly until the player goes quickly into trance upon speaking or thinking of that word. And repetitions of the word may be used by the player or the guide as a means to deepen the trance. Or, in the case of a word-image such as "butterfly," an approach utilizing the player's imagery may be used, and often this will be more effective.

Then the guide might say:

All right, say that word, and I will observe that you are in trance when I see that your eyes have involuntarily closed. Good, they are closed, and now you will look for the butter-fly, and when you see the butterfly, or have a very strong awareness of it, then nod your head. And now describe it to me, holding the image, and you will be learning to go deeper as you hold the image and make observations of it.

And now you will see, and in the future you will see, that the butterfly is moving away from you, so that you have to follow after it to keep it in sight, but it flies slowly enough so that it is not difficult to follow. And, as you follow, going deeper.

Going deeper, the butterfly moving off across a little field, and into a woods, and there are beautiful flowers to see and to smell, breezes to feel, and the birds are singing, and the path in the woods slopes down now, down and down as you go deeper into trance, and that is the path you will take on occasions when you want to do that.

Going deeper, and it is darker in the woods, but a very

comfortable darkness, and the butterfly appears to be luminous and even more beautiful, glowing and becoming more and more beautiful as you watch and follow after, and keep going deeper and deeper. And now just keep going where the butterfly leads you, at the same time going deeper and deeper, until you feel quite certain that you have been taken just as deep as you are going to go at this time, and I will know you have reached that point, because your head will slowly nod up and down.

You are there, in that deep place, and you will be able to go back again, with the word-image butterfly. But remember, and understand this completely, this image and word butterfly will not affect your state of consciousness in any way except when you intend it, and it cannot affect you in any way except when you want and intend it. Do you understand me? Good, and that is how it will work in the future, and now you will restore yourself to a refreshed, alert waking state by counting from twenty up to one, and at one, opening your eyes, clapping your hands, and saying loudly and vigorously: *Now, wide awake!*

Having been given such a key word, players will be urged to work with it often in the days ahead until they have learned to use it well.

The method used earlier by the players, of writing in an imaginary notebook, also is a good self-induction technique, and includes a deepening procedure. Guides and players may invent their own inductions, until each player has learned to alter and deepen consciousness, and to move from one depth level to another.

In any group of players, it always will happen that some will show a much greater facility than others for going easily and quickly into the ASCs, and some of these will also show a greater ability to reach those profound depths in which the greatest range of capacities become accessible and the richest experiences and applications of the capacities are able to occur.

Some players always will learn less quickly, and some players will be slow in learning to respond to deepening suggestions. A certain number will demonstrate considerable resistance to going into trance at all. But every player, with persistence and training, eventually should be able to learn to achieve altered states and to go deep enough to have most of the experiences which the mind games make possible.

Another minority of players will achieve early those very profoundly altered states which are called somnambulistic. And the guide should be alert to detect these fortunate and talented persons, since they may have especially important contributions to make to the playing of the mind games.

Those somnambulists, while in a profoundly altered state, are able to perform any task they might be able to perform in the ordinary waking state, and to many observers will not be recognizably in an altered state at all. However, in trance, they have a greatly increased ability to concentrate and observe closely, and are alert to some very subtle nonverbal cues. They also have access to a considerable range of mental capacities not available in the ordinary waking state, and this often seems to include an unusual awareness of the thoughts and needs of other persons.

In the training of players who experience difficulty achieving ASCs, somnambulists should be assigned to observe those persons during ASC inductions, and they will often prove able to suggest inductions that will be effective. They also may be able to deepen trances of players who have been resistant to deepening. Because of these exceptional talents, somnambulists in a group should be encouraged to become as skilled as possible in the induction and deepening of ASCs, and the guide should see to it that their training is as complete as possible.

Training sessions to enable players to induce and self-regulate ASCs, will continue to be held from time to time so long as there seems to the guide to be a need for them. When most of the players no longer require this, then the guide may make arrangements to work separately with those who need more training, working with these players individually or in small groups.

This game is a considerably more intense version of a game played earlier, in the first mind-games cycle.

It involves the experience of becoming an animal, and is derived from animal metamorphosis rites that have been acted out in countless times and places since remotest antiquity. These rites still are being performed today by many peoples and at places scattered throughout the world. Animal metamorphosis has been further observed to happen spontaneously in altered states of consciousness induced by mind-altering chemicals, and sometimes by other means.

The game will be played by only one player at a time. The guide will induce ASCs in all players, or request that the players perform their own inductions and deepening, and then a single player, who already has acquiesced in the selection, will be brought forward as the subject of the metamorphosis rite. Then the guide will say to the player:

Go deeper now, and for the duration of this game believe without any reservation in the facts and possibilities to be described to you.

Go deeper, and know that you contain within you elements of an evolutionary cycle going far back beyond your own life, beyond human life, and into a prehuman time, and your own genetic inheritance contains traces of the prehuman, of animal, reptilian, and other nonhuman life forms from which all human beings, and you yourself, have emerged.

Go deeper, and know that genetically coded into your body is the possibility, even now, of re-establishing contact with the consciousness of one or more of these prehuman or nonhuman life forms. And soon you are going to go back in time, back far beyond your own present life, back along the evolutionary chain, until you find happening within yourself an element of animal consciousness, a consciousness that can be and is being revived.

Feel it now, feel it happening now, and this animal you are beginning to experience will have been for some ancestor of yours a totem animal, an animal he clearly recognized to be an aspect of himself, and which he, or it may have been she, always had the capacity of becoming, through a metamorphosis, reawakening the life and consciousness of that animal dwelling within, always dwelling there from that body's first beginnings.

Go deeper, and you are going back, to meet that consciousness arising within you. And you will keep going back, through time, you are already going back now, going back far beyond your own life, and going back through the hundreds of years, going back very quickly, and deeper until that animal, whatever it may be, begins increasingly and inescapably to dominate your awareness. Gathering strength as it is being reborn now, and occupying the body that was yours in that place and time where you were when you began to play the game, and when that body was your body.

And feel it strongly now, how you are being changed in so many ways, and so profoundly and basically changed, your consciousness undergoing transformation, and your present body becoming known to that animal consciousness as the body of the animal awakening now, as from a long and profound sleep awakening, and the awareness to which I am speaking is increasingly and almost totally that animal awareness.

Becoming that animal more and more completely, but still susceptible to my commands when I give them, because there remains just the finest of threads, but an unbreakable thread of connection, to the human being you were, to the time and place where you were, and the connection, with communication possible, that fine thread linking you to me.

Becoming that animal, being that animal, but still responsive to me, and now it is time for that animal fully to emerge, and that animal exists now as a vital and indisputable reality for us all, here and now. And except for that thread, of which there will be no further awareness until I speak again, the animal is *altogether* animal, and *free*.

The guide and the players then will observe the behavior of the player who is subject of the game, and will consider the question of what animal it is and how completely metamorphosis has been achieved in terms of the appearance of the player, the player's actions, and the mentality presently manifesting to them.

After the player has been observed for a while, and depending on what may be occurring, the guide will return the player to her or his normal body image and state of mind, with suggestions that there will be a detailed memory of what just has been experienced.

The same procedure then may be followed with various of the other players.

:: *11* ::

The present mind game includes tactical exercises and navigational aids for inner-space explorers. Players should be informed that they are going to encounter a variety of symbolic forms and imaginal world situations that they will need to know how to deal with, and they are going to receive such instruction as they play this game.

ASCs then will be induced and deepened, and the guide may next speak as follows:

You will be completely attentive now to what is said to you, and to the realities arising in response to what is said.

Behind your closed eyes it is growing darker, and darker, and for the moment you will find yourself in a timeless void where nothing happens, and there is nothing to do but wait, knowing that you are in that void temporarily, and the best way to deal with this situation is to sleep more deeply, since the more deeply you sleep, the sooner it will seem to occur that you can move out of that void in which you are suspended.

And now, you will not awaken or be less asleep, but nonetheless you will discover that you are emerging, as if from a cave, and you are in a mountainous region, and you will have to climb down those steep slopes below. And now you are climbing down those slopes, surrounded by great, gray boulders, and with a lot of loose gravel underneath your feet, so that you will need to be very careful not to slip, and you are wholly absorbed in this task you have of safely climbing down.

This is what you have to do, descend, because for now it is not possible to move in any other direction, and you understand that you *must* keep going down, and down this slope, and deeper and deeper into trance, until all at once you will find yourself at the very edge of a sheer precipice, looking down hundreds and hundreds of feet, into a gorge so deep you can barely, if at all, discern the bottom.

But you do know that far, far down there are sharp and spearlike rocks jutting upward, and looking to the side of you, and then looking behind you, you recognize that it would be almost impossible to make the ascent back up in the direction from which you have come, and neither is it possible to move very far to either side, or worth the effort to try to move to either side.

You are in this situation, and it is a situation you have to find some way to deal with, and as you think about it, you must recognize that this would *usually* be an extremely dangerous and very frightening situation to be in. But *now* you will understand, and really know, that in this *imaginal* world the laws are different. And even more than in other worlds, here it is the imagination that shapes the reality and determines the laws, and as you come to know this, then you know that you will *always* prevail if only you use your imagination creatively and with confidence.

You do know this now, and as you look down into that deep, deep gorge there before you, you will know that you don't have to fall, but that you can slowly and gently drift. If you want to, you can just very gently drift down, slowly, slowly, landing with a featherlike lightness.

Or, if you really had wanted to go back up, a single bound could have taken you all the way to the top of the mountain, but then you might not have learned about some of the ways you have to deal with the gorge.

And, standing at the edge of the gorge, it might be that you could simply extend your arm before you, doing that now, and making a circular motion with your arm, inscribing three circles, and so causing the gorge, as you see, to quickly begin to fill with water, water that is quickly rising up and up, so that you could swim across to the other side.

The water rising, until you are standing not at the edge of a gorge, but just at the edge of a lake with beautiful blue water, and you will want to kick off your shoes and dip your toes and feet in the water, feeling how refreshing that water is, and noticing how extremely beautiful this place is, until suddenly your attention is focused on a disturbance in the water.

A whirling in the water, more and more turbulent, and approaching the place where you stand. Something is coming toward you, and up, rising up out of the water and approaching you, a horrible-looking sea serpent, monstrous and menacing, opening its long jaws to reveal yellow teeth like daggers. And this monster moving closer and closer, as you feel yourself now to be so frightened that, as in dreams you had when you were a child, you find yourself momentarily unable to move, or cry out, but then it occurs to you that this sea serpent is probably not truly a sea serpent at all, but some other being turned into a monster by an evil spell that some witch or magician has cast.

And having that thought, you find yourself free to move your arm, inscribing circles in the air, and then holding out both your arms to the monster, which already is changing.

Changing, and suddenly right there before you, taking your hand, just as you have decided it would be, some beautiful young princess or prince who has been bewitched, but who now has been saved by you.

Talk now with that person, and make friends with that person, and you have one minute of clock time and that will be all the time you need for this friendship to ripen and deepen, and you may spend hours, or even days together, and do that starting *now*!

I am calling you back, since we have urgent tasks ahead, but probably you will meet your friend again, and that friend may be a very valuable ally for you in the future, a strong, beneficent force within you, and appearing in dreams, or trances, or whenever needed to give you some most important help.

But now, looking off to your left, you will see, coming toward you down the rocks, a very fierce-looking mountain lion, giving every indication that it is about to attack you.

But observe, your anxiety is much less this time, and you are aware that this situation is well within your means to control, and it is just a matter of finding a suitable method of handling the problem, and an imaginative method, since just the command to "go away" may not work, and that kind of approach is not in accord with the nature and the laws of this reality.

But, you might cause to appear in your hand some food that this lion will find especially to its liking, so that you would just feed the lion, and in this same way you might want to feed any monster or dangerous beast appearing to you in any imaginal world, experienced under whatever conditions. In that way the danger may be dealt with, and you might want to make friends with the wild beast, so that the lion could be experienced as lying at your feet, almost purring like a kitten as you stroke it.

Or, if the lion still is not friendly, you could just point your finger at the lion, saying: "And now you will get smaller and smaller, smaller and smaller, right before my eyes, until you are no bigger than a kitten." And watching the lion dwindle in size until it becomes no bigger than a kitten, telling it now: "Unless you decide that we're going to be friends, I am going to just leave you like that."

Now, you will find it growing darker again, darkness all around you, and no sense of any particular place, as you concentrate on what is being said to you, and learn it, your conscious mind and your unconscious learning, and drawing out implications, as you understand that even from a few examples, you learn means of dealing with a great variety of situations that may in future times confront you.

Whether it is a matter of dealing with threatening forces, as we have been doing, or making positive, creative applications, as we do in many other of the games, you always will be learning, and from this learning you will become able to invent your own solutions and tactics, and you will get better at this as we continue with the games.

And now I am going to instruct you to return to a refreshed and alert waking state, and I will do that for you *now*!

The players will have been instructed to bring along with them to this session the dream diaries they have been keeping. Each player also will have been asked to write out in the fullest possible detail one or two dreams that are believed to be of particular importance. If a player has an interpretation of one or both of these dreams, then that should also have been written down and should be brought to this mind-games session. Interpretations should deal mainly with what the person thinks to be the meaning of the dream, as distinguished, say, from an analysis of the original sources of the images and ideas of the dream, except as the meaning of the dream cannot be stated apart from such an analysis.

The guide will induce and deepen ASCs, or will request the players to do this, if in a group all players have by now become able to satisfactorily perform the self-induction and deepening. Then the guide, from among the dreams brought to the session, will select one of the dreams and then address some player other than the one whose dream was selected. The guide will tell that player:

In a little while now you are going to find yourself having a dream, but first you will find yourself going deeper, and going deeply into a state that is just as close to your normal sleeping and dreaming state as you can achieve while still maintaining contact with me. You can go deeper now, and go quickly into that dreaming sleeplike state, and I will give you a minute of clock time, and that will be far more time than you need to reach that state.

You are asleep, and able to dream, and I am going to describe to you the dream you are going to have, but have in your own way, as it will come to you. Understand this, you will have that dream not just according to the description I will read to you, but you will have your own dream according to what your unconscious mind understands about the meaning of the dream I will read. Your unconscious mind will have a good understanding of what the dream I read means, so that your own dream will have a similar meaning, but not the same setting or characters, and your dream will be clear to you as to what it means. So, after you have had your own dream, you will describe first that dream to me, and then provide an interpretation. Do you understand?

Good, I now will read the dream to you, and when I have finished reading I will say to you: That is all, and have your own dream starting right *now*!

Later, the two dreams and the two interpretations will be compared, and the results discussed and evaluated by the group. This game may be played with as many dreams and players as the guide thinks desirable.

A second kind of dream game then will be played, utilizing a player who has demonstrated the capacity to achieve very deep trances and who is able to be amnesic, or forget afterward what happened in those trances. Such a somnambulistic player will be told by the guide:

When given the instruction to do so, you are going to have a dream, so now you will want to sleep, and to sleep just as you do when you dream and sleep at night, only still being able to maintain your communication with me. I don't know what that dream will be about, and you don't know what it will be about either, but it *will* be a complex, significant dream, and veiled as to its real meanings by much symbolism. Sleep deeply, and when your dream is ended you will make the fact known by an involuntary slow nodding up and down of your head, and you will have that dream *now*!

When the player nods, the guide will ask for an account of the dream, and this account will be recorded on tape. The player will then be awakened with the suggestion that there will be no memory of having had any dream at all. Then another trance state will be induced in the same player, and the guide will say:

In a moment I am going to play for you a tape-recorded account of a dream that someone had, and you will hear that *stranger's* voice recounting a dream that is quite unfamiliar to you, and you will be hearing that voice and that dream for the very first time. You will listen closely to the tape, and after I have played it for you, then, at my request, you will sleep very deeply and dream a dream that will clearly disclose the true meaning of the dream that I played for you on the tape recorder.

This interpretive dream of yours, which will just happen while you are sleeping, will have little or no symbolism, its meaning will be very plain, and it also clearly will give the meaning of that dream it interprets. I will play the tape for you now and when the recording is completed, I will say to you: Sleep and dream and do it *now!*

When the player signals, as arranged, by nodding, that the dream is over, then the guide will ask for a description and interpretation of the dream.

If the dream does not seem to have been interpretive of the earlier dream, or if it was partially so but some symbols still remain to disguise the meaning, then the same procedure should be followed again, with another amnesia, another trance, and a tape of the second dream being played, the player then having a third dream to complete interpretation. And sometimes a fourth or fifth dream might be needed before the meaning of the first dream has been arrived at, and the guide may want to pursue the matter that far if it is clear that progress is being made from one dream to the next.

Finally, the guide will suggest that all players sleep and each dream a dream that will express the player's feelings and ideas about the mind games, the progress being made by the person, and how the progress of individuals and group might be improved. It will also be suggested that this dream, or perhaps a dream that night or the next, will include some new mind game that might be played to the benefit of the player or of the group.

Players will be urged, as well, to dream about new means to induce and deepen trances, and they will describe these so that the group may decide if it wants to try out the dreamed games and procedures.

After termination of ASCs, the group will examine and discuss the various dream diaries, and the guide may want to keep the diaries for a while to study them and discuss them individually if the players or the guide feel that this would be beneficial.

Players will also be strongly encouraged to continue maintaining these diaries, to make them as detailed as possible, and perhaps to illustrate them with sketches of images or any other illustrative materials.

:: 13 ::

The altered states will be induced and deepened repeatedly until it is felt that a maximum depth has been achieved. Then, the players will be told that this game can be of very great benefit to them, but they must accept that it is important and to be taken most seriously, and the benefits will be greatest if the deepest possible trance is achieved by each player, so that several minutes will be allowed during which an even more profound depth now can be reached.

At the conclusion of this period, the guide will inform the players that they will now participate in a rite to be designated, "The Smashing of the Enslaving Idols."

And the guide will say to the players:

I want you to know, if you do not know it, that you have been impaired and blunted in your capacity to experience the world with your various senses, and you may not even have much awareness of the extent of this crippling.

But with each of your senses, and in varying degrees, you do experience your world as if a more or less thick and transparent substance of some kind, say a sheet of glass, has been placed between you and that world. You perceive through that glass, and so you do not experience immediately, but only as if you are separated from what should be experienced by you with immediacy and without any separation or estrangement of this artificial sort.

Know this, and now you will see before you a scene containing trees and grass and sky, flowers and animals and people, only you are able to perceive now that between you and that scene's full reality is a glassy substance that blurs, and sometimes distorts, and always prevents your complete sensing of the reality.

And understand and believe that you do not have to know what that glassy substance is, or means, or how it came to be there, and it would be a waste of your time and effort to go into such a matter at the present time, because all you really need to do is to smash through that impediment to your full appreciation and knowledge of the world available to your senses.

You know what needs to be done, and you will pick up from the ground near your feet a heavy, long-handled hammer, a kind of sledge hammer, and you will smash through that glass, really, effectively smashing at the same time through habits and conceptualizations that have impoverished your sensory world, and whatever other elements are included in that glassy substance.

Smashing that substance into small, harmless fragments, and knowing that this symbolic act of demolishing impediments to immediate awareness will carry over into everyday life and ordinary waking states, letting you experience with full intensity, so that your world will be more acutely, accurately, and pleasurably experienced by you.

More, I want you to know and accept that by smashing such symbolic forms and obstructions, one often greatly undermines, and may even altogether eliminate the power of the symbols and their power source, what they may have been expressing for the unconscious. So that you are not determined by that force any more, and there is an expansion of both your freedom and your awareness.

Understand that we all are victims of idols and of symbolic forms that express certain values and attitudes and ways of feeling and thinking that were imposed on us in the past by someone else, or developed as products of our own error. You will go deeper now, and go down inside of yourself, as through a dark tunnel, until you find some of these unwanted, detrimental symbols and idols.

It may be that one will represent a fear you have of an authority figure, a fear deeply rooted in your past, and this symbolic form when you find it might bear the face of your father, or of some teacher you had when you were a child, or you may even recognize conceptions of God that were forced upon you long, long ago.

We all contain symbols, images, idols of this kind or something similar, and they cripple us in varying degrees and in various ways. Now, I am going to give you five minutes of clock time and during that time many of these idols may rise up before you. These will be symbols of forces that inhibit you, limit your freedom to feel and to act, and in all sorts of ways have worked to prevent you from becoming what you have the capacity to be, and from having experiences you want to have and are entitled to have.

And, as these idols rise up before you as images, you will strike them and smash them, knowing at the same time that you are destroying much or all of their power to affect you any longer, and you will begin *now!*

The guide will observe responses of the players, and on that basis will announce that the ritual is ended.

Then, very slowly, and with many suggestions about the success of the rite, and about how good each player is going to feel as a result of this rite, the guide will bring the players back to an alert, refreshed waking state.

:: *14* ::

After ASC induction and deepening, the guide will say to the players:

Be aware now just of what is being said to you, and be entirely concentrated on that, understanding and learning, because this game we will play can be of the greatest benefit to you, as you learn here so that later you can make your own applications of this important knowledge.

I want you to know that pleasure and pain only very rarely must be experienced as having any necessary intensity or duration, and it is possible there is *no* necessary duration or intensity of either pleasure or pain.

And pleasure or pain may be experienced as mild or intense and as long- or short-lasting, very much at the discretion of a person, if only that person is aware that this is possible, and knows how to go about regulating these responses to stimuli. Such self-regulation has to be learned, and you are going to begin that learning, taking first the all-important step of finding out on an experiential level that such controls really are possible.

Now there is something else to be understood, and this is that in our own culture we tend to intensify pain sensations and to extend their duration. Or we tend to dilute and diminish our pleasure sensations and to decrease their experiential duration.

We do this probably, and most fundamentally, because of the belief and values systems arising out of our religious and other ideological heritage. Long ago, we believed that matter was evil and that material pleasures were sinful, and that we, as material beings, should suffer, and that our pleasures should be spiritual, and available to us only when we are freed of our bondage to the material. But material meant the world, and our own bodies, and so we learned to suffer more than we need to, and to prolong our suffering. And we learned to have less pleasure than we might, and to cut short our pleasures.

We are going to play now a game we also played during the first cycle of the mind games, but this time we will play it with capacities and understandings you have gained since then, and applications you have learned how to make. Especially important to your experience is going to be your ability to accelerate mental process, to utilize AMP.

Listen carefully now, and go deeper, feeling yourself to go deeper and deeper, and I am going to play some music for you. This recording will last, by the clock, for only three minutes. But you are going to experience it as playing for so long that the matter of duration will cease even to be meaningful. Or the duration will be experienced by you as so extended that it won't even occur to you to think any more that the experience had a beginning in time, or that it will ever end.

And, as you did on that earlier occasion, you will experience the music with your entire body, you will be touched by it, only now you have learned a lot about responding, so that this experience will be vastly more intense than the earlier one. The sensations actually will be so extremely pleasurable as to be almost unbearable, almost unbearably sensuous and sensual, stimulating in you physical pleasure as great as any you ever have known, and in duration far exceeding any pleasures you have known.

While you are experiencing this, it will be just pure experience, so you won't be thinking about it at all, but nonetheless you will be learning how great is your body's capacity for pleasure, and how extended experientially the duration of pleasure can be.

And now you are prepared and I am going to play that music for you beginning *now!*

If, in the opinion of the guide, the players are not as yet ready to have the full experience in three minutes, then the same instructions will be given except that the guide will specify a longer time, perhaps long enough for the playing of one side of a long-playing recording.

The guide may also find it desirable to play several pieces of music, after the instructions for the first piece, then just informing the players that their responses to the second will be even more intense and otherwise rich and complete than were their responses to the first music played, and similar instructions would be given with regard to the playing of a third recording.

After all the music has been played, the guide will want to point out some future applications the players may make of what they have learned, and the guide will say:

Relax now, relax for a while, and go deeper, retaining the afterglow of your pleasure, but relaxing, drained of all tensions, and feeling yourself relaxing through your whole body, and going deeper, deeper, deeper, and listening, and learning.

I want you to know, and really know, that even the most intense of all pain can be both diminished in intensity and greatly contracted in experienced duration, just by using the kind of mental capacities with which we have been working. And there are other pains it is more likely you will want to deal with, and need to deal with, and you are laying the foundation for that.

If one of you sometime should have a baby, be giving birth to a baby, and there should be a long period of labor, then that period of labor might be made to seem not very long at all, and the pain might be diminished, or even, as we have observed it to happen, transformed into sensations of pleasure. And I want to say this again, so that you will learn it even better, that even a childbirth that would ordinarily be very painful and long may be transformed by these powers of the mind, correctly applied, so that the duration is brief or of no consequence, and the giving-birth experience is pleasurable even to the point of being intensely ecstatic.

If you are in that or some other situation, you will know, and your body is learning now, that it is quite possible for you to experience pleasure and pain in these ways which will be most beneficial for you.

The guide will then terminate the altered states, encouraging a subsequent, thorough discussion of experiences and ideas.

:: 15 ::

The guide will inform the players that they are about to again engage in exercises to create a collective consciousness and to evoke the Group Spirit, first called forth in the Book One mind-games cycle.

The group will first engage in rhythmic breathing exercises, until the entire group is breathing as one, and this breathing will continue for several minutes.

The guide will instruct the players that this breathing has brought them closer and closer together, they are quickly now becoming one, and they will go into trance together to create a collective mind that will be greater than, and independent from, the single mind of any player.

The guide will join with all of the players in a five- to ten-minute chanting of the OM, and the guide will ask all of the players to close their eyes, and to feel themselves quickly going very, very deeply into trance, and there will be two minutes of clock time during which, with accelerated mental process, there will occur a deepening toward a profound depth of trance.

At the end of this time period, the guide will lead the players in chanting:

> One mind, one mind, one mind.
> One mind, one mind, one mind.
> One trance, one trance, one trance.
> One trance, one trance, one trance.
> One ever-deepening trance.
> One ever-deepening trance.

After several minutes of this chanting, and by prearrangement, a player able to function well in deep trances, a recognized somnambulist, will move to the center of the group, saying:

"Now all of you will flow toward me. Now all of you will flow toward me.

"I am the center, and you flow toward me.

"Deeper and deeper, deeper and deeper, as I now, in this deep trance, draw you until we all meet together, in this deep, deep place.

"We will go deeper and deeper together, going deeper, all flowing together, creating one mind, one trance, one ever-deepening trance.

"And out of·this collective mind will arise that symbolic

form, that entity we have called the Group Spirit, and you *will* feel it arising now, and you *do* feel it arising now, out of this one trance, out of this one mind, out of this one pool of consciousness into which flows the mind of us all.

"Feel it now. Know it now. Born of that consciousness, arising out of it, detaching itself from us now, this Group Spirit to which we all have given birth.

"Be aware of it, know its existence, and know now that *it is real.*"

The somnambulist who has given these instructions, now will call upon some other players who appear to be in very deep trances, instructing those players to become increasingly aware of the Group Spirit, increasingly in rapport with it, and to describe whatever communications are sensed as emanating from it. These same players will, for the others, serve as receivers for answers to questions put to the Group Spirit by any player who does not feel in rapport with the entity.

If there should be no communications, or when the guide feels that enough has been done, the guide will ask the somnambulists to return to the group, and all players will be told to go even deeper into trance, deeper and beyond the previous level, and as this happens each player will feel her or his trance to be increasingly separate from the collective trance.

And players will be told, at the same time, to be aware of the Group Spirit as being drawn back down into the pool of collective consciousness from which it emerged, and then of its losing force and ceasing to exist as that pool becomes dissipated, and the Group Spirit cannot exist until the pool has been recreated and the players call it forth once more.

The guide will then instruct the players that each now will be detached completely from the collective, that each player is completely individual again, separate and fully individual. And the guide will begin a slow, leisurely instruction of the players to return to an alert waking state.

Near the surface, just before the players are wakened, the guide will inform the players that on the next occasion a game will be played at which once again they will invoke the Group Spirit, and on this occasion they will endeavor to visually perceive the Group Spirit, and to give it some measure of substance.

Then the Group Spirit might be apprehended with any or all sensory modalities. This will happen if the experiment succeeds, and while playing that game the players are going to believe firmly that they will succeed.

And the guide will state that the players are being told ahead of time about what is planned, in order that both the conscious and unconscious mind will prepare, and be prepared, for the next session, and so that any player who does not wish to play this particular game will just stay away from the session, as those players should do.

After this, the guide will complete instructions for a return to a refreshed, alert waking state.

:: 16 ::

Exactly the same procedure as in the preceding game will be followed up to the point at which the Group Spirit has been detached from the collective consciousness and given, for the duration of the game, an independent reality.

The guide will then instruct the players that the Group Spirit will remain as an independent existence for a while, but will be susceptible to the controls of the guide. And it will continue to exist throughout the game, or until its existence has been terminated as a part of the game.

The players will then be given instructions to withdraw from the collective consciousness, each regaining his or her own individuality and separateness from other players, while remaining deeply in trance. And the Group Spirit exists apart from that collective consciousness out of which it came.

The guide will next request a somnambulist to stand close to the Group Spirit, and the players, remaining deeply in trance, will open their eyes and observe as this somnambulist three times closely encircles the presence of the Group Spirit, so that the presence is localized for all players, who will fix their glance unwaveringly on that location.

Players then will be told to concentrate more intensely on that location, and now to feel flowing out from themselves and into that space substance and energies which will give to the Group Spirit a degree of material being sufficient for it to be perceived with the senses of the players.

The guide will remark that it may be necessary to even further energize the Group Spirit before it becomes sufficiently material for *all* of the players to perceive it. But *some* players undoubtedly perceive it already, and others certainly will find themselves perceiving it in a moment, or very shortly after that.

And eventually, *all* players should perceive it—see it, and possibly also hear it, and be able to touch it, and the Group Spirit then might communicate with any player.

The guide will announce to the players:

This Group Spirit has been created by a version of a method known and practiced for thousands of years in Tibet, where such entities are known as *thought-forms*, or *tulpas*.

Then the guide will address the Group Spirit, inquiring as to whether a mentality embodying the collective knowledge and capacities has been created. And, if this should not be the case, then the Group Spirit will be requested to define its nature and the capacities it has. Responses to these questions may be received by all or some of the players, and one player may be designated as recipient of the communications, then relaying these to the other players.

The potentials of the entity might be tested by obtaining from it answers to questions in any field in which it claims competence. And it might be asked to endeavor to predict various future events, and about games that might be incorporated into the group's activities, so that the players' development will occur more quickly and be enhanced in various ways. And there should be questions varied enough to probe at the knowledge and thought processes of the entity.

When the guide feels that the questioning should end, players will be advised of this, and then the players will be instructed to become aware of the minds of all players flowing together again, flowing together to create one mind, one trance, one pool of consciousness, and time will be allowed for the formation of this pool to occur.

The guide will then order the Group Spirit to return to the pool of consciousness from which it emerged, and the guide will decree that the Group Spirit shall cease to exist until such time as it might be called forth again during future exercises.

After this, the guide will give instructions, as in the preceding game, so that the players will withdraw from the one-mind state, each player resuming his own separate identity.

The guide will now remind the players that the Group Spirit is only a symbolic form, a psychic construct that is being used in the mind games to test certain mental capacities of the players, and also to explore some awarenesses and potentials described since ancient times in the writings, religions, and philosophies of some other cultures.

Such experiences as the players have had with the Group Spirit deserve investigation, and inner space explorations need to venture into areas which Western psychology has neglected to study. The guide will add that the players will make a rational and critical approach to all phenomena explored in the course of the games.

The guide will terminate ASCs, and a discussion will be held.


:: *17* ::

The guide will request the players to induce and deepen a collective trance, and to go into this trance during breathing exercises and chanting, which the guide will lead.

The guide will further deepen this state by leading, or having a somnambulist lead, the group in repeatedly chanting together:

> We are one mind, one trance.
> We are one mind, one trance.
> We are one mind, one ever-deepening trance.
> We are one mind, one ever-deepening trance.

After that, the guide will call upon the players to create a work of art expressive of the collective consciousness of the players as they draw near to the end of the second cycle of the mind games.

As it was done in the first cycle, so the players will do it again.

Successive contributions will be made by the players, until the work is adjudged by the guide to be complete, and a majority of the players concur with this judgment of the guide.

Players will be told that in creating this work, they are aiming for not just a work of art, but for a symbol expressing their present state of development, and a symbol which may be used by them as an object for meditation.

And this work of art, when it is completed, will be compared with the work completed in the first cycle of the games, and the players will discuss how the two works differ, and will explore the nature and meaning of the changes, and what appears to be revealed by the differences between the two works the players have created.

:: *18* ::

The guide will welcome the players to this, the final mind game of the second cycle.

ASCs will be induced and deepened, and the players will be asked to repeat the meditation with which they ended the first cycle of the games.

In this meditation, the player is represented by a series of concentric circles, the number of these circles being determined by each player, as the image of the circles comes into consciousness.

Each player will ask, beginning with the outer circle, "Who am I?" and will find that a symbolic image emerges in response to the question.

And the player will continue asking, "Who am I?" and, in so doing, will keep moving inward and inward until the center of the circle has been reached.

It is understood by the player that each move inward, each successive circle, leads the player toward the center of the circle and a symbol that will be the deepest and most comprehensive self-symbol the player is capable of achieving at the present state of that player's development.

When the symbol of the innermost circle has been reached, a player, remaining in deep trance if possible, will open her or his eyes and will draw, with materials available for this, a picture of the deepest, most comprehensive symbol, and then of the other symbols apprehended during the meditation, moving from the innermost on to the outer circle and symbol. Or, if the player cannot draw the symbol, then it will be described verbally.

And this record of the accomplished meditation will be compared with the results of the meditation performed at the end of the first mind-games cycle, and the player will reflect upon this comparison and endeavor to understand the changes in the symbolisms in relation to personal changes that are felt to have occurred.

Then, members of the group might join together to evaluate or try to discover the meanings of the changes in the symbols and how these relate to recognized or apparent alterations in the behavior or values of a person, or any other changes in the person that may seem to have taken place during the playing of the games.

This same measure will be taken again, at the conclusion of the third and fourth cycles, and the records should be kept for these future comparisons.

Finally, the guide will congratulate the players upon their performance and upon having reached the end of the second cycle. Players will be assured of the value of the games, and that each player is accomplishing something of value to himself, to other members of the group, and for mankind by contributing to the general understanding of the human mind-body and its capabilities.

And the guide will say:

Strengthened by all that you have done, you are prepared now to undertake a new, more difficult, more challenging series of mind games, and you will find that these games also are more complex, and they will take you deeper, deeper, into more profound and mysterious realms and dimensions of experience.

And the guide will terminate ASCs, after that once again congratulating the players for their accomplishments.

*Mind Games:* BOOK THREE

## A Special Note to Mind-Games Players:

Mind Games Three demands of the players skills and understandings and kinds of experience they will not possess without having successfully completed the earlier mind-games cycles of Book One and Book Two.

Those games were a necessary preparation, as the Book-Three games are an essential preparation for the more demanding games of the final cycle, to be set forth in Book Four.

Players must be able now to go deeper, and otherwise to penetrate into regions of awareness remote from the surface of consciousness and also going beyond the previous experience of the particular player.

Those who are ready may go very far, breaking through to antipodes of the mind, realms of archetypes, of essences, pools and whirlpools of psychic energies, powerful dynamisms never or rarely ever encountered by the player before.

Awareness deepening, and spiraling out, with the depths and the larger dimensions experienced as one.

If the player is ready, the games, successfully played, will lead into ways of knowing and being not accessible to the player before.

Such a player will reach not an end, but an opening. There is always more, and still More.

Go deeper now,
and deeper,
as you play
these games.

*How to read to learn mind games:*

Whether the reader is reading as a preparation for playing and guiding the games, or may be reading for some other purpose, the reader, if not having done so before, should allow these words that the eyes and the mind-brain are focusing on to be the whole content of consciousness.

Being conscious only of what is being read, just that, so that participation will be greater, so that the learning will be more complete. What is now learned will be thoroughly learned, with understanding on all the mind's levels, and taking deep, solid root, becoming a lasting part of you.

And what is being suggested to the reader is not an effort of concentration, but that the reader make *no effort*, only just *relax*, simply *let go*, and experience the words rising into and filling consciousness.

Then you will be gently borne along by them, and the words will easily rise up as images, so that when you read about a mind game, you will visualize that game clearly, and have clear images, too, of sounds, smells, taste, and touch sensations, sensations of movement, almost as if *you are there*.

As you *do* learn to *respond* that well, you will be participating in the games, *learning* to be a responsive player, and guide, and *already experiencing* something of altered states of consciousness, or ASCs, experiencing *trance*, and learning to *go deeper*, so that you can experience and learn *even more*.

*You really can* learn to respond, and *go deeper*, and so be able to learn much better all that is being taught in the mind games, *letting go* with your body and *responding* to the invitation and instruction to go *deeper, deeper*, until the sensations of *going deeper* are felt by you, and then you *know you are doing it*, and you are *completely* involved in the words, and in your response to what is being said to you.

And the more you read, the more you will know, about

ASCs, about trances, about going deeper. Learning, perhaps without even recognizing at first that it is happening, how to go into ASCs, and how to go deeper, as it is taught in the mind games, as it is learned by playing the games and even, in many cases, just by reading, as you are doing now.

As you can do it now, relaxing, relaxing, and remembering what it is suggested that you remember, and not doubting at all that what you are told to remember really happened, really happened to you, although you may have forgotten about it a long while ago.

Remember, and accept without doubt that it is true, that when you were a very small child, there was a dream you used to have, having it over and over, and you may need to be reminded of some of the details of that dream, and then you will know that you really did have that dream, and it was important for you, so that you had that dream very often.

At night, when you slept, as a small child, in a bed you are about to remember, the same dream, recurring again and again, so that you were not sure if it was a dream, although it was not your usual waking reality either. But it was more like going into another world, than it was like your usual dreams, and so it had a special kind of reality about it, as you will remember more and more clearly.

And beginning always in the same way, as, in the dream, you believed you were awake, and dreaming you were awake you would get out of your bed, walking across the room to the closet, and finding that there is a door in the back of the closet. A door you never could find when you looked for it when you were awake and not dreaming, although sometimes you did look and look for that door, looking for sliding panels or buttons to push, or something that might cause that door to open.

On those past occasions when you were not dreaming, the door never opened, but now, in this dream, the door does open for you, so that you pass through the door and then stand at the head of stone stairs leading down.

It is a very ancient-looking stone staircase, winding down and around, and in the dim light you begin going down the staircase, not at all afraid, but eager to go down, deeper and deeper, descending on down through the dream, going always deeper as you go down a step at a time, until finally reaching the bottom of the stairway to stand at the edge of what you recognize to be dark water, as black as ink or cypress-swamp water, making a lapping sound, where a small boat is waiting.

And now, resting on blankets in the bottom of the boat, the boat adrift and floating in the blackness, dark all around, but rocking gently from the motion of the water, back and forth and rising and falling, rocked gently as the boat just drifts on and on, and as the boat drifts down and down, as you feel only that gentle rocking, listening to the lapping of the water, smelling a pleasant smell of the dampness, and then becoming aware that the boat is moving toward a light in the distance, then passing out of a cavernous opening and into a warm sunlight.

Still floating downstream, feeling the warm sunlight, and a soft breeze that passes caressingly over you, as you drift down and down, and along the bank the birds are singing, insects are chirping and humming, and the fish are jumping in the water to the left of you, and then to the rear. There comes to your awareness the smells of the flowers, and of the freshly cut grass in the fields, where the mowers still are working.

And you draw from these things feelings of great contentment, serenity, drifting drowsily down and down, down and down, with that gentle rocking, and now just let yourself feel it all for a while. Be aware of this whole situation, the movements, the warmth, the sounds, the odors, as you keep drifting on down and down, down and down.

As a small child you dreamed it, and perhaps you remember now that you dreamed it, or remember dreaming something else, about getting out of your bed, and going somewhere, out through the back of the closet, or out by some other way, but getting up out of your bed and going into another reality, a reality more real than any you usually experienced in your dreams, and to which you returned, over and over again. The dream described to you, or another, but very vivid, very real, so that remembering back into that dream, you experience once again the child you were, and the dreams as you then dreamed them, and the vividly imagined worlds, subjective realities, magical, trancelike awarenesses you had, recollecting those states of consciousness, letting those states now occupy your mind.

And you do this not to become a child again, but as an aid in recapturing possibilities that child had, capabilities that child had, and lost for a while, but not irretrievably.

The mind games are, of course, retrieval procedures, and the reader who has been able to respond to the reading of the games by experiencing ASCs has taken important steps toward reopening doors, regaining access to inhibited or forgotten capacities. Readers who have not yet responded, may do so later, or they may require the stronger stimulus of participation with other players in the games.

Those readers who *have* responded to the text, now have the choice of terminating the present state, or of maintaining it, the better to respond to the accounts of the games in the third cycle. Readers who have responded but do wish to terminate ASCs now, will look at the image below, clap their hands vigorously three times, and speak aloud the words below the image.

If the situation is such that the reader cannot clap hands or speak aloud, then it will be sufficient to vividly imagine so doing. These actions will effect a return to the reader's "normal waking state."

The same actions will achieve the same results in the case of ASCs resulting from reading the mind games to follow.

Wake up!

On the occasion of this first session (if not done at a pre-liminary meeting), players will select the first of those persons to serve as guides during the third mind-games cycle.

The guide thus selected then will choose as his assistants two persons, preferably one of each sex, who are capable of achieving deeply altered states, and of being able to carry out guiding functions while in those states. Most groups of any size will by now have such players, but in the event a group does not, the guide will select as assistants two players the guide especially values for their sensitivity to the needs of other members of the group. These assistant guides, when not guiding, will participate along with other, nonguiding players.

Before beginning to play the first game, the guide will welcome the players to the session, congratulating them on what they have achieved up to this point, and advising them that a very great deal still remains to be done.

Players will be invited to join in a period of rhythmic breathing, and then in chanting, as an affirmation of the group's unity of purpose and harmony of feeling, as together now all players are going to begin again to move deeper, deeper and beyond the regions and experiences hitherto probed. Deeper and deeper, through the unfolding of the mystery they have come together to explore.

The guide then will induce, or players may self-induce, a trance which then must be deepened until all players have reached the maximum depth of which a player is presently capable. And the guide will say to the players:

As these words come into your awareness, feel the heaviness of your limbs, the heavy warmth of your body as it settles—lethargy, drowsiness, coming over you, and a profound relaxation, as your body settles, as the trance moves through your entire body, so that you definitely feel this trance all throughout your body.

You are entering a state that is closely related to a very deep dreaming sleep, a profound sleep in which it is possible to be aware of other realities, and these might be only subjective and private, or they might be something else, indefinable, unknown.

And, in just a very short while, I will call upon you to experience something that for hundreds, even thousands of years, was one of the most important and beneficial of all human experiences, a means of healing if one needed to be healed, but also a means of maturing and growing, a way of coming closer to enlightenment.

It was the custom for these thousands of years, that a person would go into a temple, and would sleep in that temple for a night, and during that night there would come to the sleeper gods or other entities possessing greater than human powers and wisdom.

And the sleeper having come for that purpose, these beings would examine and assess the sleeper, and determine what needed to be done, to effect healing, or to activate those natural forces and dynamisms able to propel that person on toward self-realization.

These gods or entities would come to the sleeper in a vision, what might seem to be a dream, activating those energies and mechanisms which, then, would continue to function for as long as might be required, and the sleeper would awaken to some degree transformed.

For thousands and thousands of years this practice was carried out, and it really did happen that way, a very, very powerful and good experience that had some most beneficial effects on the person who underwent this temple sleep, or incubation, as it was called.

And you should understand now, and thoroughly believe, that it is still quite possible to have that same experience today. The same capacity still resides within us, and those same forces or beings, those symbolic forms, still may effectively be called upon to perform their ancient and powerful rite. They *will* appear to perform the rite, and the rite *can* be experienced successfully, *really can and will be* experienced successfully and within the context of the mind games.

Go now, again, deeper, and deeper, and deeper, going ever deeper, beyond all particulars, space, time, deeper and deeper, aware only of your responding to these words given you to help you to reach and for a time dwell in that beneficent and eternal place.

Going deeper, continuing deeper, until you find yourself to be in a temple, a temple out of time and in sacred space, and you will be greeted here by robed figures, figures whose faces seem to be lost in shadows, and even if you glimpsed them for a moment they will be forgotten by you, and you must follow those figures.

Follow them, and they are going to lead you, are leading you down a very long corridor, down the corridor, and down and down, to that circular room containing only, in its center, a slab of stone upon which you will lie, and sleep profoundly, so that the rite may be performed.

And taking your place there now on that stone, surprised at how comfortable it is to lie there, and remarking how terribly, terribly drowsy you are feeling now, all at once, and beginning to drift away into deep sleep, aware as you drift off into that sleep of those hooded robed figures who brought you to this place, that they are withdrawing like shadows from a room over which descends a heavy, warm darkness that covers you.

You will sleep now, and sleep very, very deeply, very profoundly asleep. So that, in a moment, even my voice will not be able to reach you any longer, as you carry out the instructions I will give you now in these last few moments before you sleep so deeply that you will be aware of nothing but the content of your dream.

And during that dream there will come to you those gods or entities who, for you, will be best equipped to do what needs to be done, to activate within you those energies and mechanisms having the power to transform you in some important ways.

You know now that they do have this power, you believe

and know that they really do have it, that they will be able to exercise the power, that you will really experience this ancient, ancient rite and its effects.

You are going to experience the rite completely, in all its timeless power and profundity, and in your own extremely deep sleep, aware only of the content of your dream, that sleep blotting out all else, and that dream beginning *right now!*

The guide will carefully observe the players and will allow them sufficient time to have their individual experiences of temple sleep.

These experiences will typically seem to the player to have a duration of hours, if not of an entire night, and yet will rarely last for more than several minutes as measured by the clock.

The guide will not give any specific instruction about how much clock-measured time will be needed, but the guide will *expect*, without saying so, that only a few minutes of clock time are going to be required. And in no case has it been observed that any player, under these conditions, has taken more than fifteen to twenty minutes to complete the incubation or temple sleep. But this does not mean, of course, that no exception ever will occur.

And these experiences will be very different from one player to the next, the guide having only created a basic situation within which a practically infinite variety of events might take place.

At the end of this game, when all players have been restored by the guide to a refreshed, alert waking state, then the players may compare their experiences, and the diversity should be brought to the attention of the players, illustrating the point that the guide does not control or give the experience, but only helps to create conditions enabling an experience to occur.

Players will be encouraged to discuss their experiences, and instructed that the player should record her or his own experience in the personal diary that will be kept for all of the games of this third cycle.

It should *not* be *required* of any player that he or she discuss what happened during the temple sleep, or during any other mind games in which deep psychic levels may have been probed, intimate and private matters dealt with, and psychic processes made active that a player will want to integrate quietly and reflect upon, not discuss prematurely and perhaps interrupt.

The purpose of the mind games is never to compel any player to make revelations to the group, and each player's privacy is respected while, at the same time, the group is available to share and discuss what a player wishes to disclose.

:: 2 ::

Altered states of consciousness, or trances, will first be induced by the guide, or induced by the individual players, and deepened, and then the guide will say to the players:

Your awareness is narrowing now to include only the voice that is speaking to you, and certain aspects of your body, the heaviness you now feel in your limbs, the warmth that goes with the heaviness, and the outline of your body, so that you have an image of your body within its outlines, but beyond those outlines there is nothing.

There is no time, there is no space, there is no here, there is no now, so that it no longer matters at all whether time is space or space is time, or whether there is here, or now is then, or here is then, or where now is, or where now was, and, in fact, you will feel your awareness of your body's outlines becoming blurred, and you are losing the sense of your body, and losing that, until you are aware just of this voice that speaks.

You are pure mind, just pure awareness, consciousness out of any context, focused entirely on this voice, which is going to remind you that although you presently have no sense of your body, you do have a body of which you have no need to be aware. But it still exists, and it functions without your having to be aware of it functioning, looking after all the necessary tasks, while you listen only to what is being said.

And you will know, and well understand, that from the

very beginning of your life you have been absorbing countless impressions, been assimilating immense amounts of knowledge, storing ideas, symbols, every kind of information, and you have been creatively processing these data on levels mostly out of consciousness. So you really possess amounts and varieties of knowledge going far beyond any knowledge to which your conscious mind has ever had access. And, moreover, your unconscious has worked with this knowledge creatively, and the products of all that work are within you, constructs of your mind which properly belong to you, but have been unavailable to you.

Go deeper now, and know that experience has taught us ways of gaining access to much of this material, and also other knowledge, knowledge you would seem to have been born possessing, knowledge inherited by you and coded into your genetic structure. There seem to be ancient memory traces, going far, far back beyond your own life, and perhaps going back beyond all human life, into distances of time too remote for you to try to comprehend. And you seem to be linked to those remotenesses, and to bear within you images and other traces which, if fully understood, might unlock secrets and mysteries never fathomed by contemporary minds.

And more, your unconscious appears to have access to knowledge which is neither coded in, nor has been received by you through any means of which we now know. This knowledge that the unconscious mind knows, appears to be gained from a kind of reservoir of images and other knowledge of a culture or a people, a pool of images and symbols and other elements which feeds into the unconscious minds of individual members of the culture or people.

And existing in the unconscious there are found to be symbolic forms and archetypes, including beasts and gods and personifications, sometimes encountered in myths and in dreams, and in altered states of consciousness, ASCs variously induced or just spontaneously happening. And these archetypes, when brought into awareness, may know much of what the unconscious of the person knows, and much that the person's conscious mind did *not* know. So that by bringing one of these archetypes, these symbolic forms into consciousness, it sometimes is possible for the conscious mind to learn what the unconscious knows, and this knowledge can be of very great value.

Go deeper again, and deeper, and know that one of the symbolic forms existing within you and able to bring you such knowledge, has been called the "wise old man," and this wise old man does exist within you, and can be brought into your awareness.

Continue to go deeper, and as you do go deeper, you are drawing closer to the wise old man, who will manifest to you. And you will become aware now of a gathering darkness, and, as your trance deepens, you are aware of being on a road and struggling up and up along the road, and you are taking this direction up, even as you go deeper into trance, so that the wise old man will be able to speak to you at the highest level of development you have yet achieved, and you will keep climbing up until that is possible.

Moving up, climbing up through the darkness, until the darkness starts to lift a little, so that you can make out rocks lying on the road, and going up and up and up, and going deeper and deeper into trance. And you should know now, and understand, that in trance sometimes you reach a point when you find that having gone down and down, always going deeper as you go down, it happens that even as you keep going deeper, in geographical terms it will seem to you that you are going up and up.

You will feel strongly that it is just such a thing that is happening to you right now, as you keep climbing, not finding it too difficult to continue making this ascent. Going deeper and deeper into trance, as you go up and up along the path, and you will catch a glimpse in just a moment of the place you have been climbing toward. It is a little house at the top, and within this house to which you feel yourself drawn, and drawn more and more strongly, lives the wise old man.

Going up and up, approaching the house, and at the same time deepening the trance, until you reach the door of the house, and knock, and wait there for the wise old man to open the door and invite you to come inside of that house.

You are going to be able to stay with him there, and speak

with him at considerable length, and ask him anything you might want to ask. But you will have to be completely open and honest, holding back nothing, since that would be pointless and he already knows much more about you than you yourself are aware of, and he understands you much better than you understand yourself. So it would be self-defeating not to be completely open, since anything short of that will put needless limits on what you can ask, and will distort all you say. Just keep in mind that what you would like to have from this wise old man is the benefit of his very great knowledge and wisdom, and you want his answers to the most important questions you are able to ask.

In just a minute, I am going to leave you for a time with this wise old man, and I'm going to make sure that you have all the time you could possibly need for your conversation with him. I am going to give you seven minutes of clock-measured time, along with the suggestion of accelerated mental process, AMP, as you have learned it and thus are able to respond without any conscious effort to the suggestion. And this means that, subjectively, you will have available to you all the time you need, and this can be hours or days or even whole weeks of time. It will be however much time you need to ask the wise old man any questions you can think of concerning your own life, your goals, and the best means of achieving those goals. And you will have this conversation with him beginning right *now!*

At the end of the seven minutes of clock time, the guide will inform the players that if they have not completed their conversation with the wise old man, to do so now, and to say good-by to him, and to remember everything that has been discussed during the conversation with him, so that when they sit down later to write in the mind-games diary, they will have a very good recollection and be able to record it in detail.

And the guide will add the following:

Before terminating ASCs, one further thing should be pointed out to you, and you will pay close attention to my words, and you will understand those words, and you will act accordingly.

When you read and think about your account of your conversation with this symbolic form, you will make a reasoned, critical analysis of what was said to you, and you will do this with the firm knowledge that you are not dealing with revealed truth, but with ideas and images and facts that may be erroneous, and that may or may not be of value to you. You have been exploring a *possible* source of important information and insight, but as with all materials brought back by you from subjective worlds and realities, there must be a subsequent weighing and testing, and the value must be demonstrable.

The purpose of mind games is to enable you to come closer to making use of your whole mind, the whole range of your potentials. Reason and imagination, especially, must not be used antagonistically, but must be brought together in creative collaboration. Also, conscious and unconscious minds, to use those terms in a loose, popular way, should collaborate within the harmonious whole that is you.

Even if you do not realize it now, you do understand what is being said to you, and more and more you will operate according to that understanding. More and more of your mind will be used by you, and the different processes, mechanisms, and strivings will work together in an increasing harmony and with greater effectiveness, as you develop your powers and become increasingly a whole, unified personality and self.

:: 3 ::

The guide will announce to the players that what can be a very powerful and important experience has been scheduled for this occasion. The game to be played opens up the possibility of new dimensions of intimacy between persons. The game must be played with a partner, and those who want to play should now find a partner among the other players. When those who are going to play have paired off, they will be seated with the partners facing one another. When this has been done, the guide will continue the instructions.

Players will be told that one member of each pair will induce a trance state in his or her partner, and then deepen that state, using the familiar method in which the player is told to imagine a notebook and pen and then is told to imagine writing the player's name, and trance, over and over again until the player feels that it is time to begin writing deeper and deeper, until the deepest possible trance is felt to have been reached, when the player will lay the notebook and pen aside, informing the partner that this point has been achieved.

The player inducing the trance will then advise the partner that this trance will be terminated, but that the same trance depth can very quickly be reached again in just a little while, when the player is simply told: "Go into trance now, quickly into trance, and go deeper, deeply into trance, just as deep as you were before." After· that, the partner will be counted back to a waking state.

Next, roles will be reversed and the identical induction and deepening and instructions for re-entering trance will be given to the other member of the pair, after which that trance, too, will be terminated.

When all of the pairs have completed this process, the guide then will say:

And now, those of you who wish to do so, you will go deeply into trance together, and you will share that trance and have experiences together on levels of consciousness almost impossible to share by any other means. And if you want to do that, you will give one another the prearranged induction and deepening, just saying to your partner: "Go into trance now, quickly into trance, and go deeper, deeply into trance, just as deep as you were before." One partner first giving these instructions, and then the second partner, after having responded to the suggestions given.

And the guide will explain that, during this game, each player will give from time to time additional suggestions to the partner to go deeper still. The players will increasingly be aware only of one another and the experience they share, with the sole exception of being responsive to the guide should the guide have a question to ask them, and also being responsive to the guide in this way: when a player feels the guide's hand on his or her shoulder, then that player will slowly withdraw from the *shared* trance, ceasing rapport with the other member of the pair, but remaining in an altered state and being responsive to the guide. And, after that, the player will continue to be responsive only to the suggestions given by the guide, and not in any way responsive any longer to verbal or nonverbal suggestions or other communications from the previous partner in the shared trance.

The guide will further explain to the players that when one of the players, after the inductions, has achieved a clear image of some place considered to be a good starting setting for the shared trance, then the player should describe the setting to the partner, and invite the partner to try to come to that place, so that the joint inner space exploration might begin from there.

And when the players feel that they have found one another in the trance, then they will begin to speak to each other, describing just what is being seen or felt or otherwise experienced, and determining with the partner to what extent the exploration is in fact being shared.

As an aid to a more complete sharing, the partners may numerically designate trance depths, perhaps along a scale of from 1 to 100, with a signpost to indicate each of the depth levels. Then, for example, if one player is at level 60, the partner can be so advised and encouraged to try to come to level 60 also, after which the two might go deeper together.

In some cases where partners feel that they have gone into very deep levels together, they may find that it seems possible to stop speaking, and they will be able to continue on together and feel that communication is at least as complete as before, although no words are being spoken. As an aid to this kind of communication, which may be experienced as telepathic, the players should make some physical contact, probably by holding hands.

Players will be told to be aware only of their shared experience, while remembering to respond to the guide in the ways the guide already has described.

Having given all of these instructions to the players, the guide will inquire of the players if they understand completely what is to be done, and if they completely acquiesce in their agreement to be responsive to the guide. The guide will further elicit from the players their pledge to behave responsibly and with good will and high ethical standards toward the partner in this game.

The guide will then instruct the players to begin, and will allow an hour or possibly longer for the sharing of the altered states by the couples. However, from time to time the guide will inquire of a couple if both players wish to continue, and will terminate the shared trance if any player indicates a wish to stop.

At the end of the game, the guide will place a hand on each player's shoulder in turn and then give instructions to each of them that the player should return to an alert, waking state.

Having done this with each of the players, the guide will then very quickly induce ASCs in all of the members of the group, he will deepen those states, and will advise the players that they are now in a trance in which the relationship is exclusively a communication between guide and player, and that each player is responsive only to the communications of the guide.

The guide will then say to the players that they will have a full memory of what occurred during the shared trance. They will have learned a great deal about how to function in the context of a shared trance, and they will be able to do this better and better if trances should be shared on some future occasions.

The guide will then terminate the ASCs, and the experiences during the shared trance states will be thoroughly discussed. The guide will also be available after this game to any player who might feel the need to discuss the experience privately.

Players will discuss means of improving all procedures, and of enriching the shared trance experience. And the meanings and possibilities of sharing of ASCs by two or more persons will be examined as fully as the players might desire.

Guides, in preparation for this mind game, will study the instructions until they are familiar with the entire sequence and have understood why various instructions and procedures have been set forth. Guides will rehearse the instructions to the players until familiar with the sequences and well prepared with the instructions to be given to their groups.

Such advance rehearsal by the guide should always be made, but it is especially essential for this and certain other more than usually complicated and detailed games.

:: *4* ::

The guide or the players themselves will induce and deepen ASCs, and if this is done by the players, then the guide will continue with deepening suggestions after the players have gone as far as they can go by means of their own suggestions.

After a while, the guide will suggest to the players that awareness be totally focused and intensely concentrated on what is being said and what is going to be said, and the guide will then address the players as follows:

It has always been so, from the most ancient times, that the visionaries, the explorers of imaginal worlds, those individuals who have penetrated the deep symbolic realms of the personal self and the psyche, and perhaps gone even beyond that, have eventually encountered archetypal figures, symbolic forms, that seem to have the definite function of being guides, figures that, once having entered awareness, are able to lead the person who will follow the guide on down into deeper and deeper realms.

The guide leads deeper, and if one follows, there may be a movement down into depths wherein are revealed mysteries of the normally unconscious life, and these guide figures sometimes even lead the person into and through initiations or other rites that may be of considerable importance as vehicles of growth, or means of moving toward greater maturity, self-understanding, and wisdom.

Listen to me now, and hear me carefully, when I say that what I am able to do for you, and will do for you in just a few moments, is summons up for you various of these guide figures, and it then will be up to you to decide whether to accept the experiences these figures might afford you.

What those experiences might be, neither I nor anyone else can tell you. You will follow the guide if you want to, and that figure will lead you into some region of your mind-body where you will have an experience of unpredictable content, although I can say this to you, that if you trust the guide and have confidence in the ability of the guide to protect you, then you will be safe from harm.

And you must follow the guide, if you do follow, with the certitude that the guide is able and willing to help you move ahead on the way of growth and enlightenment. You should also remember what you have been taught about symbolic forms and imaginal worlds, and how to function in subjective realities, since those lessons have been an important preparation for experiences of the kinds you may be about to have, depending on your own choice.

It is time now, and you will be aware first of all of a darkness that even now gathers around you, becoming darker, and darker.

And you will feel yourself being transported, deeper and deeper down into a cavern, the blackness illumined by shimmering and rippling waves of golden light, becoming bronze, becoming silver, as you now stand upon a heavy stone pavement enclosing a circular pool of black water, shimmering and rippling and reflecting silver light.

Look at the center of the pool of black water, there is a turbulence, something is rising, something is rising up toward the center, rising toward you, and you will feel now that whatever emerges out of the pool, it will be something from which you have nothing whatever to fear, no matter how formidable its appearance might be.

And, as you watch that swirling silvered black water, the light within the water intensifies, and the water is becoming clear, becoming crystal clear, so that you can look down, and down, and you see that the surface turbulence has been caused by something from very, very far down, very deep down, that only now is rising into view.

Rising, coming quickly to the surface, and emerging up from the water, you perceive now an enormous crocodile, and it is emerald green, scales glowing as if they are precious stones. The great crocodile, circling the crystal-clear water, and moving toward you, its immense jaws wide open, and as those jaws yawn just before you, you know already what it is that you must do.

You know it, and you will do it, and now you do go forward into the mouth of the crocodile, crawling, and you crawl down into its belly, the jaws closing after you, and you are aware that the crocodile has dived back down into the water.

I can go with you only a little further now, tell you just a little more of how you will begin this journey, as you go down, and down. And, somehow, you will be able to see what is happening outside the crocodile as this descent is made. The crocodile descending, deeper and deeper, deeper and deeper through water you will become aware of now as waters of time. Down through the waters of time, and you will know that you are passing layer after layer upon which stand ruins of ancient cities, ancient civilizations, forgotten places of which contemporary man presently has no inkling at all, although these places once existed and belong to the history of mankind upon this earth.

And the crocodile will carry you deeper and deeper, until finally you will find yourself in a place where there is no more water, and the crocodile will open its jaws and you will crawl out and advance toward whatever is awaiting you there.

You will advance toward that experience, knowing that, when the time comes, the crocodile will return you to that place where you were when the crocodile first appeared to you, and when that has happened then your head will involuntarily fall forward and move backward, fall forward, move backward, fall forward, move backward, three times, and I will then know that you are ready to communicate again with me.

And now, you will have to proceed alone, finding yourself now at the edge of the pool, with the silver light on the water, and you are just at that moment when the water will clear and, in a moment, the crocodile-guide will appear to you, *for the first time*, and you will have five full minutes of time as measured by the clock, and that will be all the time you will need to have hours, or days, or weeks, or just any amount of time to have your experience in the *other* reality, and you are at the edge of the pool, and the guide is about to appear to you, beginning *right now!*

At the conclusion of the five minutes, and all players having completed the experience, the guide will say:

And now, remaining in your altered state, but going deeper, you will soon find yourself on a road that passes through a valley, and that fertile valley is on your right, but on your left is a steep cliff, rising almost straight up, and as you stop and stand there in that road, you will see approaching you and halting before you an immense turtle.

It seems an incredibly ancient turtle, a turtle that has been since the first turtle was, and on its back a chair has been placed, a chair in which you will now be seated. Settle yourself in that chair, and look down, and all around the edges of the shell of the turtle observe the huge rubies glowing, as if a beautiful fire burned inside each one. And, just inside that outer ring of gems, notice the golden symbols inlaid, mysterious symbols, inscrutable to you, and yet you cannot fail to recognize the power those symbols possess.

Meditate now on a blazing gem, and after that on a golden symbol, and, as you do that, the turtle will take you into a forest glade and there waiting for you will be a wildly beautiful white stallion with flashing eyes, as if lightning bolts could fly out of those eyes. Standing on the back of the turtle, you will just be able to mount the stallion, and the stallion will carry you to whatever place it is that you now must go.

You have four minutes of clock-measured time, and that will be all the time you need to have hours or days of experience in the realms you will visit, and you will go into that experience, beginning right *now!*

At the end of this period, the guide will instruct the players to return to the place of the mind games, and will tell the players that in a moment a third guide is due to appear.

And this guide will be an enormous black cat, standing erect and walking like a man, a cat with unblinking golden eyes, its heavy metal collar studded with jewels, and the cat will extend its right paw, pointing the way the player is to go.

The cat's paw points to a door in a wall, and it seems that the wall may enclose a garden, or a park, since there are trees on the other side of the wall. The player will advance toward the door, and pass through it.

The guide will allow four minutes of clock-measured time for this experience and when it has been completed, the guide will say to the players:

And now you must be prepared to go deeper and deeper, into the fourth and most mysterious, most profound realm to be investigated during this game, being led once more by messengers and guides assigned eternally to their task.

You must go deeper now, and deeper, going ever deeper until you will perceive advancing toward you, standing erect, three humanlike figures, wearing curious suits of leather armor, and with steel gauntlets fashioned to resemble the talons of fierce birds.

And, as they draw closer, you will see that these figures have, in fact, heads of hawks, with fearsome glistening, piercing eyes, and one of these bird-headed figures will take its place on your left, and one on your right, and the third figure will take its place several paces ahead of you, and they will lead you through corridors emblazoned with vast and intricate metallic shields and tablets, beautifully and intricately inscribed with complex symbols and what appear to be hieroglyphs of a civilization unknown to you.

You will go very deep as they lead you, into a hall of enormous dimensions, and in this hall will occur the final phase of the mystery you will explore.

There will be five minutes of clock time for this, and that will be all the time you could possibly need to have an extended and rich and profound and very powerful experience, and whatever kind of experience you are going to have in the place to which these guides bring you, you will have it beginning *now!*

Finally, the players will be told that they will remember all of these experiences, and remember in complete detail, so that the entries can be made in the mind-games journal.

Players will be told that any and all of these guides may be experienced again, should a player feel a desire or need to go back into those places such a guide has taken that player.

The mind-games guide then will terminate ASCs, restoring all players to a refreshed, alert waking state.

:: 5 ::

Players will first be instructed by the guide to self-induce ASCs, and then to self-induce deepening, and to continue with deepening for what may seem a very long period of time, although only three minutes of clock-measured time will be consumed.

At the conclusion of this period, the guide will again exhort the players to use their most effective techniques for going even deeper into trance. Three minutes of clock time are to be allotted, and this interval will be even longer subjectively than were the preceding three minutes. Each player will go very deep, and if a player has reached maximum possible depth, then the player and the guide will know it because the player's right hand and arm will involuntarily levitate, being raised part or all the way above the player's head.

At the end of this period, the guide will take note of which arms were raised, and will say:

All right, and now your arm will drift gently down, and you will feel it moving down even if you were not aware of it as having raised.

And you are going to find that you can go deeper still, your whole body going deeper, feeling, knowing yourself in the deepening, sensations of going deeper and deeper, as you *listen* only to my words, and hear those words spoken at what seems to be a normal, ordinary rate of speech, although your own mental processes are accelerating rapidly, accelerating tremendously now, so that you are going to be able to have a most extraordinary amount of subjective experience within only very small amounts of clock-measured time.

You are going to use this AMP you have learned, and you are going to use it as one of the elements of the creative process, as you experience your own creative process working without any conscious effort on your part, and yet in a controlled way, but unconsciously controlled. And your unconscious mind will respond to the suggestions I am giving you now, and will do the creative work to be assigned.

And what is going to happen is that, within just one minute of clock time, you are going to experience the creation, by your own unconscious mind, of a kind of short story, fully developed. You may experience this in visual images, and perhaps other images, as if it were a short motion picture, or you may experience it in some other way, but in any case you will find it to be a coherent, imaginative little story or vignette. You will enjoy its emergence very much, enjoying and being surprised at this story, not in any way trying to create it, and it will be entirely new to you and, moreover, will not resemble any story created by you in the past. It will seem to you, when you later consider it, to be a piece such as you almost certainly never would consciously create.

You have one minute of clock time during which you will experience that story, and you will start *now!*

Players may be instructed to repeat this game several times, also practicing using AMP to rehearse a task, to solve a problem, and to create a new mind game for the group.
The guide then will say to the players:

You now have learned more about accelerated mental process, and about the unconscious creative process, learning especially that this process is not necessarily undisciplined, or beyond your control, but that you may be able to specify what you want from it, and receive into consciousness something on the order of what you specified.
Your body-mind is learning about these capacities, how best to elicit and apply them, and this learning will continue as you gain better and better access to these and others of your potentials and learn all the ways that they might be used and how best to use them. You are learning all of this, and it is important and valuable for you to play these games.

The guide will instruct the players to remember and record their experiences in their journals, and then the guide will terminate ASCs.

Stories created while playing this mind game frequently are lengthy and, when recorded, fill several typewritten pages, even more. Their quality is approximately that which the author would achieve by a conscious, creative effort.
A story created during one of the games, and which is brief enough to reproduce here, is the following, experienced by the player in a little less than one minute of clock time:

"I was a tree and a lot of people came while I was growing up and sat down under my branches. This went on for a very long time. Then one day I was cut down. I was sawed into planks and these were built into a house. Eventually the house fell down. One of my planks was used by a woodcarver for making a woodcut painting. I hung on a wall for a long time and spent a long time after that in a junk yard. I became a splinter and went into someone's hand."

In the case of the foregoing little story, the following exchange then took place between guide and player:

GUIDE: How long did this sequence seem to last?
PLAYER: Well, it was like watching a movie that took about half an hour.
GUIDE: You saw it like a film?
PLAYER: Yes. But I could also feel it. I especially felt being cut down and going into the man's hand at the end. I saw through my leaves and felt most of the things that went on. There was the music of birds around me all the time.
GUIDE: When the tree was cut down did it experience pain?
PLAYER: No, just a feeling of falling.

:: 6 ::

The players, altered states induced and deepened, will be told by the guide:

I am going to describe a scene for you now, a place you are going to visit, and an event you are going to participate in, but first you will just listen to the description, not going there or being a participant until you are instructed to do so.

Go deeper now, and when I do instruct you to do so, you will find yourself proceeding along a path in the jungle, not lost in the heavy, lush vegetation, or concerned about the teeming wildlife of the jungle, but somehow knowing how to proceed, although you certainly never have been here before.

And you're going to come to a clearing, where a very powerful ritual involving chanting and drumming is being performed by primitive people. This is an extremely wild and elemental rite.

You will perceive it first as a spectator, seeing the fire in the center of the clearing, the naked, glistening bodies dancing, hearing, and resonating to the ever-more-compelling beating of the drums, until your own body is throbbing with that beat, until you are caught up in the ritual, feeling in your body what those primitive people are doing, feeling just everything they are feeling, knowing everything they are knowing, as they dissolve the individual consciousness of the participants in the ritual, creating one collective consciousness.

And you will be totally drawn into that, becoming part of it, a part of the totality of this ritual experience, and you will have ample time to experience the entire ritual, and you find yourself on the path to that ritual, beginning *now!*

When observation indicates that the players have completed experiencing the rite, then the guide will say:

Remember now, remember completely, all that you have experienced here.

Remain deeply in trance, and now go even deeper, and, as you go deeper, return to this place from whence you started.

Go deeper, aware for the moment only of the words being spoken to you. And now, those words are going to transport you, and you do find yourself being transported, this time coming to a mountainous region that looks as if it might be somewhere in Tibet or Nepal or India.

Wherever it may be, you do know that you are very high up in the mountains, and approaching a temple, a large stone temple with steps leading up, and you are now ascending those steps.

Going deeper in trance, and ascending those steps, and entering into this ancient temple. Inside the temple, you observe that there are monks, a group of monks who have come into the temple to sing and to pray.

And these monks will sing the music developed by their order over thousands and thousands of years, a music that *is* prayer, a music that has the function of making an immediate, direct contact with God. So that these monks, as that singing rises upward and outward, experience their God coming to them through the music, and this is a very, very powerful and beautiful music for you to hear.

And as you keep listening, you will experience something of what they are experiencing. Give yourself over completely to that music now, open yourself up to that experience, and you will do that starting *now!*

The guide will allow ample time for this experience, and for a period of assimilation, and then will gradually terminate the altered state.

As the terminating instructions are given, the guide will intersperse suggestions that the players will remember in detail, and will later write down their experiences. The guide also will suggest that before the next meeting, each player will have a nocturnal dream, and in this dream she or he will revisit either the people in the jungle or the monks in their temple; this will be a very vivid dream in which more will be learned about the peoples visited and about the meaning of the experiences had with them both in the trance and in the dream.

One player's experience of this game was described by her in part as follows:

"Having reached the jungle clearing, at first I was standing off to one side, kind of watching and making mental notes about what they were doing. Then I was doing it with them because it was a sound that just went all around and in me and out of me. I was doing it with them and they were dancing. My body wasn't dancing but it was into all the rhythms that they were into.

"Then they were sitting. There was a silence and they all sat, they all fell down kind of, they didn't sit slowly, but instead they all fell down into sitting positions. They all kind of curled up into themselves and put their heads down. Everybody had their eyes closed but it didn't matter, you didn't have to look or touch anybody because the feeling was just all over, in the ground and the sky and everything.

"This feeling, it was just part of the ground and the sky and the people, and you know, there just wasn't any you and me and world around. I was just one with them and they were all one voice and one breathing together. At first I was frightened, because they were already into it when I got there, but then pretty soon I was where they were. But not right away, because they were really, really far, far out.

". . . Once before, in group chanting, I experienced something a little like this, but then there was a lot more mind in it. This was all body and skies and earth, and then it wasn't really people. For a while, you couldn't experience it as a 'we,' because there was just a one. Then it wasn't even human, it was just a physical being that I was part of."

This same player described her experience with the monks in the temple:

"I was at a distance from them. It was so beautiful, it was men's sound, so rich and full and gentle, but very deep. Not deep in pitch but deep in resonance and strength and wisdom. They all sang, there were many of them—thirty, fifty, I don't know, I never can tell numbers. There were many, and they were in very neat order, like four rows, and the sound was like rows, but it was such a rich sound. It was real movement, at the same time ongoing and yet open for what comes back along the same way.

"I wanted to know their language because that would have made it richer even, although the sound was a texture to be lost in, beautiful shape and everything, but I wanted to know what it was they were saying. I think it was very deep, very profound, very wise, very gentle. . . .

"About making contact with God, I didn't feel at all as if they were trying to break through. I felt as if they had made the contact a long time before, and that it was a very careful, in the sense of very respectful, sound. It was so much ongoing and forthcoming that they were almost saying what they were hearing as well as singing what they were saying. Like they were singing the answer and the question all at once, because it was all the same thing.

"It is a difficult thing to explain. I could share in the experience, but I wanted to share more in the message. I felt a message back and I wanted to know what it was in their language . . . but still I could understand what was happening and was profoundly with them in a spiritual way."

## :: 7 ::

The guide will say to the players:

Today we are going to play two different kinds of games, and both can be of great benefit to you. Two kinds of internal momentum will be initiated by these games, and after this session you may want to reflect on what has been done and examine the question of how the exercises are the same, and in what ways they may differ.

And now, as you have learned very quickly to do, please feel yourself to be moving into trance, into an altered state, with your eyes quickly closing, and closing tight as you go deeper, going deeper and deeper, feeling it throughout your body, and knowing that whole combination of familiar sensations, the way it feels when you go deeper and deeper, your consciousness altering more and more profoundly.

Quicker and quicker, going deeper and deeper, and using your acquired skill of AMP, accelerated mental process, using that important new ability of yours that has enabled you to have such great amounts of subjective experience within such very small units of clock-measured time.

I will give you now one minute of that clock time, and you are going to have an experience of what will seem to be very great duration of going deeper and deeper into a most profoundly altered state of consciousness, down and down into an extremely deep trance, and now *begin!*

At the end of this minute, the guide will speak, saying:

And now, if you can, you will go even deeper, finding yourself to be going even deeper, and as you do that, there will appear to you, standing before you, your own body, but becoming your own body exactly as you would like it to appear, exactly as you want that body to be, and as it has the possibility of being. Look at it more and more closely now, and it will be a realistic but ideal body image, one that you really could achieve, and one that you *will* achieve. And when you have a very clear image of your body as you would like to have it, your left hand will rise and slowly return to your lap, and you then will keep observing that image, and going deeper, until I speak to you again.

After allowing what is thought sufficient time, the guide next will say:

That ideal body image is becoming more and more real, you are seeing it very clearly, and seeing it in its full size and dimensions, and now you are going to step forward and *into* that body, you will find yourself *in* that body, so that you can try it out and make certain that it is just the body you do want to have, and if there is something you would like to change, then that change can take place.

Move around in that body, feel its strength and agility, its dynamic aliveness, its surging vitality, and make really certain that its appearance and all of its attributes are what you realistically desire. And, as you occupy that body, coming to know that body very well, your present physical body is going to be drawn into that new mold. You are moving already toward the realization of that ideal body image, and henceforth you will be doing whatever is needed to achieve that body you want to have.

It may be a matter of exercise, of eating more, of eating less, of better nutrition, better environment, whatever it is you will do, implacably allowing nothing to stand in your way, creating the conditions most favorable to most quickly achieving that body.

And henceforth that image will exist in your unconscious, existing there constantly, at all times, and it will be an attracting force, a force that will draw and compel you until your physical body and that image you have of your ideal body are as one, practically indistinguishable the one from the other. And you will achieve this, and you will really, really achieve it, and nothing that is not detrimental to your health or other well-being is going to be allowed to prevent the actualization of that coincidence of your body with the body image.

But now, put that body image and your concern with achieving the body you want out of consciousness, and it is fading from your awareness, although it will remain vivid and effective in your unconscious mind.

And you will go deeper and deeper into trance, deeper and deeper, aware only of the voice that speaks to you, and of your own experiences as you move inward, inside of yourself, moving into realms inside of yourself where your talents and capacities are accessible to you as symbolic forms and personifications.

Deeper and deeper, and into that place, looking for and finding that personification representing the talent that you have for artistic work, for drawing, or painting, or sculpting, that kind of artistic work. You will know and firmly believe that everyone has some capacity to be an artist, although in some people this capacity has been severely inhibited and may be deeply buried. All people are not equally talented, but you do have the capacity to be a much more imaginative and effective artist than you have been in the past, and you will find now that ability personified, you will find the artist within yourself.

And let that artist personality expand now, dominating and filling your whole consciousness, so that you *are* the artist, and you will be able without distraction and with the fullest access to your talent, to carry out the tasks that will be assigned to you.

And now you will be given one minute of clock time, and this will be sufficient to give you the experience of meeting in the world of images a most exceptional artist who is also a very good art teacher, and this teacher will ask you to draw. You, the artist, will draw, and then you will receive from this teacher instruction about how to make your art work more effective. You will practice, doing more drawings, receiving more criticism and instruction, and benefiting from it, and you will have all of these experiences beginning *now!*

At the end of the minute, the guide next will say:

Now you have made a beginning with these art lessons. But you want to do more, and so now you will have five minutes of clock time, with AMP, in which to go back to your teacher and spend more time, maybe several days, or a week, or even more, doing many drawings, and perhaps other kinds of work as well. Your teacher will be extremely helpful to you, and you will be learning with each work you execute, learning in rich detail, and experimenting with new forms and subject matters. And, as you execute these works, you will find yourself freer and more spontaneous, almost as if your hand now moves without any conscious direction at all, so that some of the things you create will surprise you, being things you hadn't even thought about, and you will savor this new freedom and spontaneity, knowing that you already have broken through some of the blocks or inhibitions that have thwarted your creative expression in the past. Have that long experience with your teacher, and have it starting *now!*

After the five minutes, the guide next will say:

Now you are going to have the best opportunity yet to improve your skills, to improve these artistic skills you have been developing and refining. I am going to give you, with AMP, ten minutes of clock time and that, as you know, is quite sufficient for a person to live out subjectively an entire lifetime.

You are not going to live quite that long, but during the ten minutes of clock time you will have a very rich and prolonged relationship with your teacher, improving more and more upon your drawing skills, and perhaps learning as well many things about painting and sculpting and whatever else your teacher might want to impart to you.

And you will be feeling increasingly more free, more spontaneous, and also much more confident that the artist within you is emerging and developing and overcoming inhibitions and blocks of all sorts, as well as undergoing some very intensive training and learning. And the artist really is there, and is able to create very interesting works of art, original, expressive of you and your feelings and experiences and novel perceptions, and you will know that you are going to continue to improve and develop your capacity for self-expression in art. And now begin that long, long period you are going to spend with your art teacher, and begin it *now!*

At the end of ten minutes, the guide next will say:

Good. You have accomplished a very great deal. And when you go home at the end of this session, or just as soon as you possibly can do it, you will make some sketches. And as soon as possible, tomorrow at the latest, you will begin a book of drawings and you will keep on working in that book, including many of the images and symbols and feelings that have emerged and will continue to emerge during the playing of the mind games.

But know that it is of very great importance for you to do this artistic work soon, and to continue with it until the gains of this session have become entrenched, gains both in breaking through creative blocks, in stimulating the imagination, and in learning. And you will feel the need to do this work soon, and you will do it.

And now you are going to become aware of the fading back into proper proportion of the artist personification or consciousness. But, when you are doing artistic work, know that this artist consciousness may emerge and come to the fore again, thereby minimizing distractions within your personality and allowing you to function artistically most freely and effectively. And, when you no longer require it, then that artist component of your personality will again recede until once more needed.

You will understand that other capacities within you also may be personified and brought forward in a similar way, and this is something we may want to do with other capacities of yours in the future.

For now, you will know and feel certain that you have made important gains here today, that much has been set moving within you and continues to move, as you continue to develop, realizing more and more of the potential that you have, becoming the fully human being that you have the potential to be.

## :: 8 ::

After ASC induction and deepening, the guide will instruct the players to recall that throughout history and up to the present there have been individuals who seem to have been able to somehow penetrate the barriers of time, persons seemingly able to foresee and describe events that for ordinary people had yet to occur. Whether the future really is foreseeable by anyone is debatable. But, for this mind game, a belief in the possibility of foreseeing future events will be programed into the players.

With this preliminary statement, the guide will request the players to go into trance, finding their eyes to be closing, and going deeper and deeper, deeper and deeper, and not doubting now or for the duration of this mind game that a foreknowledge of events is possible, and that everyone has at least some latent capacity to have a knowledge of events before they occur in the physical world and within the reality consensus.

Players will be told to go deeper and to find within themselves the place of the symbolic forms and personifications of capacities, and to find the personification of the prophetess or seeress, the prophet or seer, that capacity for standing in whatever peculiar relationship to space-time and events is required in order to perceive events not yet perceived by the reality consensus, and to allow the personification of that capacity to dominate consciousness, as one *becomes* the seer or seeress.

The guide then will say that the procedure will be to call upon the players one by one to function as prophet or prophetess, seer or seeress, and that to each person, when called upon, there will appear images of events which the person will experience as events which are to occur in future time.

Players will not want or expect to foresee events that are more than two years distant, and the seer or prophetess should endeavor to look just a little distance into the future, to make very short-range predictions, so that verification will not be too long delayed.

During this game the guide will stand ready to recognize any player who feels strongly that she or he has a real prophetic gift that is operating, and such a player will be allowed time to make a large number of predictions. Or, if the performance of a particular player seems especially impressive to the guide, that player should receive encouragement.

When all players have had an opportunity to forecast, the guide will announce a withdrawal of the temporarily imposed belief system concerning the validity of prophecy and the capacity of each person to perceive future events. The guide will suggest that players be open-minded about this as well as other possibilities of the human being which are difficult if not impossible to demonstrate convincingly. And the guide will tell the players that they should not assume that they have proved or disproved anything about precognition or prophecy, or about the relation of the future to present or past time.

Players will be encouraged to feel that they have been playing and will find themselves much relaxed and refreshed by this game, as they move now toward some much more demanding games they will play in a future that *is* somewhat predictable.

Then players will be restored to an alert, waking state.

:: 9 ::

The players will be told by the guide that they are going to have another opportunity as partners, in units of two, to share altered states of consciousness and to share together experiences on levels of awareness usually not conscious and so not able to be shared.

Players who do not wish to play this game with any partner available to them are entirely free to abstain, but then must be silent, respectful observers while the others play the game.

Other players might want to watch for a while, and then

decide to play after all, having overcome their doubts or anxieties or other cause of reluctance to participate. Such players may begin at any time.

When players who want to do so have paired off, the guide will instruct the couples that this shared trance can be more intense than the last, that they will probably find themselves able to go deeper than on the last occasion, and that they should go as deep and as far as possible while still remaining comfortable and secure in the trance situation.

However deep they go, each player will be responsive to the guide and will communicate with the guide should the guide place a hand upon the player's shoulder. Each player will affirm that rapport with the guide will be maintained and that responses to the guide will be made.

Players then will be told to induce their own trances by means of key words or whatever procedures they have found to be most effective. Each player will then deepen the trance of the partner, until each partner indicates that she or he has gone as deeply into trance as it presently seems possible to go.

Players then, by prearrangement, will wander alone for a while in whatever image worlds appear to them. And when one partner finds a place that seems an especially good place for the beginning of the mutual journey inward, then he or she will describe that place, and invite the other player to come there. When players have started to share images, or otherwise feel themselves to be together in the same place, then they will proceed together, toward whatever adventure may await them. And at suitable intervals, efforts will be made to deepen the trances.

The players will be told that they have thirty minutes of clock time available for the shared trance, and that this interval, with AMP, will allow them to have as extended an experience as whatever awaits them might require.

All of this will be explained to the players before ASCs are induced, and when the instructions are completed, the players will be told to begin.

After the ASCs have been induced, the guide will observe

the players but will not interrupt their experience at any time unless it should seem that some player needs guiding, and then it will be inquired if such is the case, and if an affirmative response is made, the help will be provided.

Finally the guide, at the end of the period, will instruct the players to return, separately instructing each player, and using the prearranged signal of placing a hand on the player's shoulder before speaking.

The player will be told by the guide to terminate the shared trance, disengaging from the trance situation with the partner, but remaining in an altered state otherwise and in rapport with the guide, and not with any other player.

When this has been accomplished with all of the players, the guide will remark to the group that no one should bring back from the shared trance experience any attachment to the partner, that the feelings a player has about the partner will be just the same as they were before this game was played.

The guide will add that players should be cautious about playing this mind game without a guide, and it never should be played with anyone about whose good intentions and ethics one is not fully confident. The guide will add that the use of shared trances to deepen and intensify human relationships surely is possible, and everyone will think of possibilities for their own relationships. However, such experiments should be undertaken cautiously, and it would be well to involve a third party as guide and adviser.

The guide will then repeat that the mutual trances are entirely dissolved and the mind of each player, on all levels, is completely her or his own.

And the guide will then terminate the ASCs.

:: *10* ::

ASCs will be induced and deepened, and the guide will say to the players:

Just for the duration of this game, and not longer, you will now know and believe that through me is manifesting an alien, intelligent being, nonhuman and greater than human, and that this entity is, with my permission, making use of my body in order to communicate with you. And, for the remainder of this game, that entity will be speaking to you, and the enormous force of that entity's mental powers will be focused on you, to help you more quickly reach your goals.

And experience me now, the one speaking to you, and know that I have the capacity to enable you to alter consciousness more profoundly than you have ever been able to alter it before. You will go much more deeply into trance than you have been able to go before, as my mind and my words exert a powerful pull upon you, pulling you deeper, and deeper, helping you to go deeper and deeper, and your development requires that you be able to go very, very deep.

And now going deeper and deeper and deeper, feeling your mind going deeply into trance, feeling your body going deeply into trance, your whole mind-body going deeper, and deeper, as you know and respond to a mental force that is greater than any you have known or responded to before for this purpose of deepening trance.

And that force will continue to pull and to draw you, deeper and ever deeper, as now you are becoming very aware of your body, of the form and the substance of your body, and finding yourself now surrounded by darkness, and knowing that your body has been somehow transported out into space, far, far out into space, where it floats in the darkness, as you keep going deeper.

Your mind is with your body, drifting out there in space, all alone except for your awareness of my voice, my words, taking you deeper, and deeper into trance, and toward important new experiences, and liberating within you capacities you have, but in the past could not use. And you will go deeper in order that you may become free.

Your body out there drifting in space, and your legs are spread wide apart, and your arms are flung out and extended, as you drift there in that blackness, as you go deeper, and now are aware of your body growing, and growing, and growing, to a size that is immense, a size so vast that you become aware of yourself as a constellation of stars that might be perceived as having human form, so that someone seeing that constellation might create a drawing of you and regard it as an astrological sign or as a figure that may be perceived in the heavens, there by accident or by the intention of some great, superhuman power.

And drifting, drifting through space now, not fixed but drifting along through the cosmos, perceiving other bodies that are also constellations of stars, and alive, some human bodies, some animal bodies, and one of these is an immense white horse, a constellation of stars but also a white horse.

And you will mount that horse, so that you might be perceived now as a constellation having the appearance of a great mythic humanoid form astride a powerful and magnificent horse of a colossal magnitude.

And riding now, riding faster and faster, across the vast reaches of the cosmos, the universe, riding in ever-expanding circles, around and around, going deeper and deeper, and becoming aware of yourself, despite your vast dimensions, as being no more than an infinitely minute cell in some organism gigantic far beyond all your powers of imagining.

And knowing this, feel yourself growing smaller and smaller, shrinking and shrinking faster and faster, a microcosm becoming where the macrocosm was, and knowing yourself as absolutely minute and alone now, the horse having vanished, alone and just a tiny cell in an organism whose nature you have no inkling of.

But becoming aware now of other cells around you, and your relationship to those cells, growing in awareness by that means, extending the scope of your being with a very fast-increasing knowledge and interrelationship with other parts of this organism, feeling yourself to be in harmonious interaction, growing in understanding, expanding toward knowledge of the total organism of which you felt yourself to be a part, and discovering finally that the organism *is* yourself, that your awareness for a time had been centered in a single cell of your own body, and that now you have become aware of your whole body and self, and that harmonious interrelationships have come to be within you, as your whole mind-body is more knowledgeable now, working more harmoniously now than it ever could do in the past.

And this is a real gain you have made, increasing harmony within the body, increasing awareness of the whole mind-body with respect to itself, and you also have a sense now of the interrelatedness of everything, microcosm to macrocosm, and now you will find yourself able to go deeper, deeper into trance, and so be prepared for the next important task you are going to perform, to free and exercise a capacity of the highest value, and we will do that now.

We will begin to do that, and you should first understand that it is not only possible to see vivid images with your eyes closed, it is possible also to open your eyes and still be able to perceive those images, but externalized, so that an object or a whole world can appear before you, and surround you, and be perceived by you in just the way you ordinarily perceive what you call external reality, out there.

And there have been cultures in which no person was considered fit to be called an artist, until the imagination of that person was sufficiently developed so that the images could be externalized, and in the case of an artist projected onto some surface to be painted.

It also has always been claimed by some that when the visionary faculty is very highly developed in a person, then that person is able to look around and see actual objects of perception which, however, are invisible to nonvisionaries. And it is claimed, as well, that visionaries may be able to perceive realities which co-exist with ours and in some sense overlap our reality in space-time. You can be open-minded about these possibilities, but what you can be certain of is that it is possible to externalize images and that this can be done by a perfectly healthy person and that a really healthy person should have access to this capacity.

But all of us have been deprived of this capacity, or it never was allowed to develop, and to liberate it and regain its use will be more difficult for some than for others.

Go deeper now, and keep going deeper, drawn just as deep

as you now can go, and remaining in that deep state, slowly open your eyes and look over here at me. As you do that, you may see your guide, or it is possible that some of you might even be able to perceive me, as I manifest through your guide, and know what my appearance actually is.

But look over here, remaining in trance, and if you are in trance you and I will know it because your left hand and arm will involuntarily rise, drifting up and over your head, as your unconscious mind advises me about your trance by controlling the arm, which you do not consciously control at all. And now your left arm will slowly sink back down, and if you perceived not just your guide, but me as I manifest through your guide, then your right arm will involuntarily raise, and move on up above your head, and then it will lower.

Close your eyes now, and keep going deeper, and whether one or both of your arms or neither arm raised up in response to the questions, just forget about that and keep going deeper and deeper, your whole body going deeper into trance, your whole mind-body going as you respond to me, and I will allow somewhat more of my mental force to manifest, as much as is safe for you now, and enough to move you very deeply into trance, as you go deeper now.

Every breath will take you deeper, every heartbeat will take you deeper, every passing moment will take you deeper, and you will continue to experience the deepening of your trance. And you will remain in that deep trance as, in a moment, and slowly, you will once again open your eyes, and you will see that you and I are together here, you will just see that you and I are together, just seeing that as you open your eyes, and look at me, and look around.

And if you perceive that just you and I are here together now in this place, then your left hand and arm will involuntarily rise above your head. And if, looking around, as I tell you that just you and I are together here, it seems to you that someone else is also present, then your right hand and arm will rise.

Letting the hand and arm slowly drift down, and going deeper, and your eyes closing, and going deeper, and just resting there for a moment, and then going deeper and deeper again, you will just rest and then go deeper, just rest and then go deeper, and you will keep doing that until you are requested to stop, and then you will stop and listen.

All right, and now for the duration of this game, you will know with certainty that there are other dimensions of reality overlapping your reality, and that it may very well be possible for you to perceive one of those other dimensions rather than your own, doing that in this profoundly altered state, and with confidence that I will enable you to regain apprehension and normal perception of your own dimension of reality when the time comes that that is desirable.

But you may be able, remaining in this trance, and opening your eyes in just a moment, to break through into that other dimension, and if you do that you may encounter intelligent life forms and possibly be able to communicate with them by some means. But whatever is there, you will be able to observe it and explore it with all of your senses, if you do make the breakthrough. And open your eyes now, and if you have crossed through, then stay just where you are, but hold up your right hand.

The guide then will select from among the players who have raised their hands, one whose experience is likely to be of particular interest, and the guide will say to that player, calling her or him by name:

Now, ———, be aware of my holding your arm, and when I withdraw my touch from your arm, and until I touch you again, you are going to be aware of nothing in your previous world, not even of my voice. Just being aware of nothing in my dimension until I touch you again, taking hold of your arm, and I will call you by name, and you will hear me, and I will be your only contact with the reality from which you came, as you go forward to explore this *other* dimension into which you have broken through.

The guide will release the arm of this player, and then will move from player to player, telling the others who have raised their arms that they will come back to their own dimension, but will be able to return to the reality into which they have broken through. And those players, and all of the other players, will be told to be awake or in a light trance, and to observe what is going to be experienced by the player chosen for the demonstration.

The guide will then return to that player, calling her by name and taking hold of her arm, and then will invite that player to begin to explore the world in which she now exists. She also will be urged to try to send out feelings of love and friendship, so drawing other life forms to her and so trying to establish good relations with those forms if she does encounter them.

This more advanced type of visionary anthropology will be observed for as long as the players want to pursue it, and the player in trance desires to continue, and it may be possible for the visionary anthropologist to bring back songs and dances and accounts of laws and economics and politics, or flora and fauna, or whatever else may be observed. And any information that might be of value to the group or to anyone.

Finally, the player will be told that it is time to end the present exploration, but it will be possible for her to go back and resume it later on if she wishes to do so, and the guide will assist with that effort. The player will be told that she is returning, and an involuntary raising of the arm will signal a complete re-entry back into our own dimension.

All players will be told that by this experience their powers of imagination have been enhanced, and their creativity, and that the benefits will continue to accrue and the capacity develop, even though no player will externalize images except under very special conditions and safeguards, and when the person wishes the images to become externalized.

The demonstration subject will be completely wakened from her altered state, and then the group as a whole will receive suggestions for returning to an alert, waking state, with the added suggestion that they will recognize that the guide is just the guide, and the belief system concerning an alien intelligence manifesting through the guide has been terminated with the ending of the trance. Terminated at the same time, is the programed belief about overlapping dimensions or worlds.

Altered states having been induced and deepened, the players will be told by the guide:

This game we are gathered here to play may be frightening at first. But it may also provide you with important answers concerning your main purposes in life; what, at its end, you would want your life to have contained and meant; and what you really believe yourself to have accomplished and been in your life, as you have lived it up to this present point in time.

Go deeper and deeper now, and continue to feel the trance as it deepens, knowing that feeling you have learned to recognize as the deepening of your trance.

And remaining in trance, and going even deeper, those of you who *know* that you have the capacity to open your eyes and perceive the externalized image that I will suggest, you will open your eyes and just sit there, awaiting the suggestion about what you are going to see.

And the other players, eyes remaining closed, and going deeper and deeper as I speak, you will wait now and in just a moment you will perceive the suggested image, and it will be extremely real for you, and it will be your whole reality except for the small fragment of awareness that links you to me and to my communications.

And I address each one of you now, every player who is gathered here, and that image is about to appear to you now, and it is the image of your own body in death, your body, and dead, and you will observe your body in death and meditate upon it.

It will be as if the meditating consciousness is that of the spirit of the deceased person, as if it is the spirit meditating, and it is *your* spirit taking a last look at the body in which it dwelt throughout the life you had upon this earth, and you do take that last look now.

You look at your body reposing there, and inquire:

"What did this person's life mean?"

"What did this person do that was of value, and how much did this person fail to do that ought to have been done?"

Going deeper and deeper, and reflecting deeply as you look at that dead body, that completed life on this earth, that finality of a life on this earth, a life that can be looked at in its totality because it has ended and nothing can be added on now, and nothing taken away or in any manner changed.

And reflecting upon that life that is now a closed book, an accomplished and unalterable fact, inquire of yourself what you would do if that dead body could be brought back to life, if the book were not closed now, and if the mistakes still could be remedied, and if what was left undone now could still be done.

And know now that in fact this is so.

You are not dead, and you do still have time in which to fulfill all of your possibilities.

You do have time to achieve what you know must or should be achieved, and time to make amends and correct the important mistakes you have made, and to right any wrongs that you know you have done.

And before your eyes now, the image of that body, that dead body seen as an image of your body lying there in death, will slowly lose what appears to be its fleshly substance, becoming as a shadow, dissipating as wisps of smoke, and disappearing altogether.

This occurring, you will become very powerfully aware of the life in your physical body, of energies, of vitality, of strength, of the life-force in your body.

You will have a sense of reopened possibilities, of renewal, of knowing that there is still time to do what you now know that you want to do, and you have motivation, impetus, to do those things, and to make of your life what it ought to be.

Resting now, your mind-body at rest, your eyes closed but not seeing any images, and your mind becoming very quiet, when I tell you to begin, you will have a minute of clock time and that will be all the time you need for your mind to completely empty out, only silence with no thoughts, no images, as on a very deep level beyond thoughts and images there occurs a mobilizing within you of the impetus, the impelling force that will enable you to become what you have the capacity to be. And then, finally, after a long, long while, into your mind there will come a sense of this force, this direction, and the conviction that you really will be able to do those things you want to do and must do, and that you really will do them. And have that minute of clock time, and that experience just described to you, starting *now!*

The guide will then return the players to an alert, refreshed waking state, and there will be a discussion of this mind game as variously experienced.

## :: *12* ::

The guide will say to the players:

Once again, as in the previous mind-games cycles, the time has come to create together a work of art expressive of the present consciousness of the group.

We have agreed upon the kind of work to be done, the materials have been brought here and are ready, and now each player will successively contribute something to this work of art, and will continue contributing until the work has been completed.

Before we begin, there are a few things to be said to you.

This work will embody and express the spirit of us all, individually and collectively.

And, as you carry out this creative work, you will almost certainly find yourself in an altered state of consciousness, and you will be aware of the deepening of that state.

There will be no formal induction, but you probably will notice that it is happening, and you will find that the trance is deepening as you work and as other players work, finding yourself going deeper and deeper so that the work expresses not just our conscious mind and minds, but other psychic levels as well, expressing much more of us, coming closer to being a total expression of us than could happen otherwise.

And you are likely to become aware of the emergence of a group self, and of a pool of consciousness to which we all have contributed, and of the work of art emerging out of that pool, as well as through us.

You will be aware of these things in silence, and from the time you are instructed to begin, no player will speak to any other player, and your awareness of the physical presences of the other players will be quite minimal.

You will be keenly aware of the work of art as it grows, as it emerges from us all, as it builds toward completion.

You will have no sense of the passage of time, or of being in this particular physical space. And we will create here, out of time and space as we usually experience these, an expression of ourselves that is independent of anything in our external environment and undistracted by it, as we go deeper and deeper, creating, and completing this work of art.

And when it is completed, we will know that it *is* completed, and we will seat ourselves in a semicircle in front of it, meditating on it and arriving at our own interpretations of its meaning.

After we have meditated a while, each player will find that his or her eyes are closing, and for a minute or two the player will experience a dream or sequence of images, also interpreting the meaning of this creation of ours.

When that dream has ended, then the guide will give your suggestions for termination.

You will remember all of these instructions, and now we will begin to create our work of art.

:: 13 ::

This game will be played on an occasion when, by prearrangement, each player is going to be able to withdraw to a solitary place, preferably in a natural setting, there to fast and to be alone for a period of twenty-four hours.

Before departing, the players will meet with the guide, who will also experience the fasting and isolation.

The players will be asked to self-induce and deepen ASCs,

and to indicate by an involuntary levitation of the left arm to shoulder level when it is felt that the maximum depth that is presently possible has been achieved.

Players will be told to lower their arms, and the guide will suggest that they now can go deeper, go deeper still, deeper and deeper, as awareness is limited exclusively to what the guide is saying, and they will continue to go deeper while the guide is speaking.

And the guide next will say to the players:

We are nearing the end now of the third cycle of the mind games, and in a little while you will leave this place to perform an exercise and discipline that can be one of the most important and developmental experiences you have had up to this time.

You will remain in absolute solitude, and you will have eliminated—insofar as that is possible—any chance that you might be interrupted or intruded upon. And you know that should your solitude be broken, you will have to repeat the experience.

You are going to fast, and this means that you will take into your body only water to drink, and as little of that as you are able to take in without being distracted by your thirst.

And during this period, neither will you sleep in the usual sense. But, from time to time, if excessively drowsy, it is permissible that you suggest to yourself the experiencing of two minutes of sleep as measured by the clock, but, with AMP, that this will be all the sleep you need, and you will emerge from it very refreshed, awake, and able to continue with your work.

Very importantly, during the whole of this twenty-four hours or during as much of that time as seems possible for you, you will remain in an altered state of consciousness, calling yourself back to a waking state perhaps every hour or so, but then immediately reinducing and deepening trance.

One main purpose of this twenty-four-hour-period of isolation will be to allow you to gain a new mastery and greater control over your own states of consciousness, and especially of the depth of trance. As an aid to self-regulation of depth, you may imagine a scale of one to two hundred, or possibly a wider scale, and you will practice moving to different points along that scale which measures your depth of trance from a very shallow one to an extremely profound one hundred, or whatever the numbers are that you have chosen for that deep end of the scale.

During the isolation, you will suggest to yourself that you will progressively recall and revivify each of the games that you have played, re-experiencing images, emotions, states of mind that you have experienced in the games you have played up to now, and you will suggest to yourself the experiencing of image sequences revealing to you more about the meaning of some of those experiences.

You will meditate, at different levels of trance, on fundamental questions, such as: Who am I? Where am I going? Why am I here? What are my goals? How can I best achieve them?

Answers to these questions may come to you as visual or auditory images, and possibly as both. Or there may be answers that are silent thoughts; arising from no specific source you recognize. And you may be addressed by some symbolic form, as during these many hours of isolation you meditate on those questions, and you also reflect upon the nature of reality, and of consciousness, and upon many other fundamental questions concerning yourself and the world.

At times, you will practice emptying your mind out altogether, being aware of nothing at all, no thoughts, no images, no sensations, nothing at all.

And at times you will meditate on images, letting the images rise up and flow, aiming for a point at which you will go beyond images into whatever state of awareness and experience is going to result for you then.

And during all of this time you will know, and remind yourself on occasion, that you are consolidating and integrating not just your experiences in the mind games but all of your experiences throughout your lifetime, and believing that you will emerge out of your solitude to some degree transformed and expanded and freed from some of your former limitations.

And you will come down from that mountain, so to speak, bringing with you insights and a new resolution that will strengthen you in the games still to be played and for your lifetime.

Each one of you will go now, having first self-terminated your altered states of awareness, and you will go as quickly as possible, and directly, to that place you have chosen for your isolation.

And, once there, you will without any delay begin the unique and essential experience you are going to have, and it will be a very valuable experience for you.

And you will terminate now your trances, and then you will leave without speaking to one another, and without speaking to me, and, for the group, I wish you success in this undertaking.

:: *14* ::

The guide will assist the players in reaching depths of trance as profound as possible, until each player indicates by an involuntary falling forward of the head that he or she can now go no deeper.

Players then will be instructed to perform the concentric circle meditation also performed at the conclusion of mindgames cycles one and two.

This meditation leads the player inward, through progressively more profound and comprehensive symbols of the self, until, at the center, the deepest and most comprehensive self-symbol is uncovered.

All of the symbols met with during this meditation will be remembered and recorded by the players in their journals, and comparisons made with the symbols occurring in the earlier meditations.

Having told the players that they will remember, and record the symbols both verbally and as drawings, the guide will inform the players that they have completed the third cycle of the mind games.

And the guide will say to the players:

You have done extremely well, and much progress has been made.

Important forces have been unleashed within you, creative energies, entelechies moving you toward a greater maturity and growth and ultimate self-realization.

Your progress will continue, you will achieve more and more, as we ready ourselves now to begin the fourth, most difficult, and most profound cycle of the games.

And now, as a preparation for that cycle:

I suggest to you that tonight you will have a very vivid and most significant dream, a dream indicating to you what your deepest feelings about these games may be, and in what ways you have been changed by the playing of the games, and what your further, most urgent needs are, and your most profound wishes.

You will remember this dream, and write it down, and it will be the opening entry in the new journal you will keep as a record of what next is to occur.

And the first guide chosen for the fourth cycle will discuss this dream with you if you want to discuss it, but the dream will not be made known by you to any other player.

The guide will then terminate the altered states, once again congratulating the players on the completion of the third cycle, and looking forward to the next gathering, when the fourth and final cycle will begin.

*Mind Games:* BOOK FOUR

# A Special Note to Mind-Games Players:

This is the fourth and last of four cycles of mind games presented in four books of mind games.

We reaffirm now what has been stated in a note to players included in each of the three preceding volumes:

To be able to experience completely these games, and to be able to realize their benefits, it is essential that the mind games be played in the order given.

This means working through all of the games, from the first game of the first book, on through the final game of this fourth book. The same order should be followed by those who want to read about the games, but do not intend to play them. If the reader does not follow this order, the reader will not fully comprehend what is being said by the authors to readers.

Working and reading through all of the games in order is a necessary practice because earlier games lay foundations for later ones, and the games have been created to move in the direction of increasing richness, depth, and complexity in the dimension of the experience of the player when the game is played.

It is also the case that the benefits of the games do not result from individual games, but the benefits accumulate and grow, as the player moves through all of the games, developing and gaining access to new ways of being and knowledge not accessible to the player before.

Go deeper now,
and deeper,
as you play
these games.

*Guiding Book Four mind games:*

The fourth cycle of the mind games should not be used as a training ground for new guides. To do so might deprive players of rewards which by now they have worked very long and hard to achieve.

However, it still is desirable that several persons serve as guides for this cycle, so that no one forfeits the opportunity to be a *player* of these games, so that there is some variety of guiding, and so that there are developed more skilled guides able to function on the deeper and more complex levels of experience and awareness.

The training of competent guides is, of course, one of the most important objectives of the mind games. With a sufficient proliferation of guides, there will be no stopping the movement to unblock and unlock the potentials of the mind, and to apply productively the vast human resources barely tapped until now.

Guides for this fourth cycle of the games should be among the more mature and knowledgeable of the players, the relevant knowledge being in such areas as philosophy, psychology, mythology, religion, literature, and the arts, and firsthand as well as theoretical knowledge of altered states of consciousness and ASC phenomena.

By this time, most players will have adequately learned to go into trance, and to go fairly deeply into trance, although they may still learn more about going deeper as these games are played.

However, greater depth will by this time probably result from experiences determined by the content of particular games, and not just by induction and deepening procedures having no other purposes.

Therefore, the most effective guide for the fourth cycle is

likely to be a person who has demonstrated outstanding skills in working with individuals who are in altered states—as distinguished from persons whose best skills lie in the area of inducing and deepening trances.

Frequently, both skills do not belong to the same person, although it always is highly desirable for a guide to have both abilities: excellence at deepening and inducing ASCs, and excellence at working with those states once induced and deepened.

We stress this distinction because it is important and very often overlooked.

Finally, a group must be mature enough, and have enough enlightened self-interest, not to make of the selection of guides a political or popularity contest, or a source of conflict within the group, or a disruptive emotional force within individuals.

By the time this fourth cycle has been reached, there can be no criterion for selecting a guide other than maximum effectiveness as evaluated by all the players.

*Trance and the reader:*

In writing these books the authors have frequently made use of what we call subcortical linguistics—a language that speaks primarily to subcortical brain mechanisms, so inducing altered states of consciousness, trances, or hypnoid states in many readers.

And many readers by now will be quite familiar with the altered states that occur from time to time as they read the mind games, and of fluctuations in depth that occur, depending upon various factors.

These reader ASCs may heighten participation in what is being read, although there may be a greater than usual difficulty in some cases in remembering what has been read, that material fading quickly, as so many dreams do. But, unlike dreams, the reader may refer back to the book for what was forgotten.

As we noted in the first book of the games, these trances, ASCs, and hypnoid states should prove relaxing and beneficial, and in some cases suggestions will speak directly and forcefully to the unconscious, so that some of the benefits of playing the games may even accrue to some readers.

However, should a reader wish to terminate a trance state induced by the reading of the book, the reader will be able to do this by looking at the WAKE UP! image provided below —looking at the image and, at the same time, clapping hands loudly together and also speaking, vigorously, the words WAKE UP!

Should it be impossible for a reader to clap hands together and speak out loudly, then it will be enough to vividly imagine so doing.

This exhortation to yourself to WAKE UP! will take you back into your ordinary state, your cultural trance, or what is described sometimes as an "alert, normal waking consciousness."

That is the state in which we all dream the same dream, at least more or less, and call it: reality.

Wake up!

At this opening session of the games, the players will select the first of the guides who will conduct the fourth cycle.

The guide will select as assistants, if available, two somnambulists or persons able to move about and function very well while in deep ASCs, and preferably one of these assistants will be a female and one a male player.

The guide then will welcome the players to the opening session, and will congratulate the players on having completed the previous three mind-games cycles.

And the guide next might say:

Through all of the experiences you have had, you now have readied yourselves to move into more expanded and also more profound dimensions of awareness, there to have experiences more powerful than you could have fully accepted and perhaps even endured without the efforts you have made as preparation.

In the games to come, there will be the possibility of extremely powerful experiences occurring, including some which may resemble or be the same as those traditionally called "satori," "samadhi," "nirvana," "cosmic consciousness," "mystical experience," and others apprehended as experiences of "ultimate reality," and of the "integral level" of the psychedelic experience.

Powerful, expanded, and intense states of consciousness, and the effects of these can be extremely beneficent, with important breakthroughs and advances in the player's development and movement toward self-realization.

There can be no guarantee, of course, that anyone will have so profound an experience.

There can be no guarantee that some players will not believe their experiences to have been more fundamental and powerful than it is likely they actually were. Then, the experience could impede progress, rather than further it. But the guide and the group will be available to help assess apparent breakthroughs and "peaks," and in some cases a player may also wish to go outside of the group for additional opinions and advice.

Your experiences with the games you have played are a valuable aid in helping you to cope with all subjective realities and experiences of deep psychic and possibly spiritual dimensions. They also have readied you to derive greater benefits from penetration into these deeper levels.

You have learned from the games you have played up till now not to be fearful, but to be respectful of the contents and processes of your own mind, and of the human mind-body system in general.

You know that that system, as yet barely tapped, has resources that are awesome and probably more wonderful and powerful than anything we seriously supposed to be the case.

We will respect that power, as we have done in the preceding mind-games cycles. We will approach it carefully, not too quickly, and always with the important safeguard of applying reason to phenomena and manifestations often referred to as irrational and, in some cases, better, metarational.

In this way we keep moving together toward that effective collaboration of reason with imagination which humanity never has achieved, but absolutely must achieve in order that the human may survive. And you will not try to consider that statement, but when you go into trance, in a moment, your unconscious mind will draw it down out of awareness to be considered on deeper levels in terms that are not just of the human mind-body, but also cosmic and metaphysical.

And now, as you *do* go into trance, going into trance as you have learned to do, quickly, and going deeper and deeper, you will begin to assimilate and understand *all* that has been said to you here. Going deeper and deeper, and assimilating, and understanding, because it is *very* important for you to assimilate and understand what has been said to you.

Going deeper, and still deeper now, and understanding

better and better. Understanding fully, and at all levels, *all* of the meanings summed up in the words spoken to you here today.

And I will give you now, in just a moment, three minutes of clock-measured time, and subjectively that will be quite time enough, and more than enough, for all of those meanings to be understood by you, to take root in the nervous systems of your body, and the brain, and the blood, down into every cell, and taking a firm root there.

And motivating you to move toward personally achieving the highest degree of self-fulfillment possible for you now and as these games continue to be played. And that learning process just mentioned to you, that lengthy and effective whole-body learning process, to be accomplished during the allotted clock time, will begin *right now!*

At the end of this period, the guide will ask the players to terminate their own ASCs, and, when this has been done, will say to them:

Before we go away from this place today, I would like to introduce you to an experience that should be pleasurable for you, an ASC induction to add to the means you already possess of opening Other Place doorways. And it might also take you unusually deep, because it does make an appeal that is different, appealing to something perhaps not appealed to before.

And I will describe to you this method, as experienced by one mind-games player on another occasion. As I do so, you are likely to have an experience that is not identical with hers, but your own version, modified by you unconsciously as an expression of your own personality and your emotions especially.

And you have a key word for going into trance, and you will now utilize that key word, going into trance, and going deeper, as I begin to tell you about this player's method, and how she began with her own key word, which was "butterfly."

"Butterfly," and speaking that word, her eyes would involuntarily close, and she would at once be in trance. Going deeper, as she followed along after a beautiful butterfly that led her deeper and deeper down into that trance.

Until she would come to a familiar door, where there are massive stone steps leading down, and that door swinging open for her at the approach of the butterfly, and seeing then a clear light just at the threshold of the door.

And then she started *going down* the steps, passing through colors and colors and colors, and these colors progressively serving to deepen the trance, and also indicating to her and to the guide the depth of her trance. And she began by passing through that very clear light, but then *going down* through yellows, and oranges, and browns, with many shadings and nuances of those colors, going through them, and *going deeper*.

Moving *down* through greens and blues, into mauves, passing on through the mauves into crimsons, and then into *deeper* purples, passing through *very deep* purples.

Going deeply and more deeply into trance, until at the very bottom of those stairs, in the depths of the trance, consciousness altered most profoundly, passing out of the purples into a velvet black, and lying down in the velvet black, sinking down into and then through that velvety blackness, until there were no meanings to think about, just serene and intense emotion, and these accompanying the knowledge of that profound interior depth.

Staying there for a timeless while, and then coming back from that place, rising very slowly out of it, and still very, very deep, moving through the richness of the deep purple, into the crimsons, the mauves, and the blues. And then slowly, slowly, comfortably moving on up through the greens and the browns, and the trance lightening very perceptibly now.

After that, she passed through the oranges, and through the yellows, and out into the clear light. And, as she moved into the clear light, standing in front of the door she had passed through, she used another word that she has, this one for passing back out of the altered states, and to produce in herself the feeling of being very alert and wide awake, and that word she has is "gazelle."

And you now, in the event you don't have one, should select and utilize a special word, to use when you want to move up and out by that means, and you might choose, as she did, a word and image that is pleasing and very lively. That word will totally restore you to the state you were in before you went into trance, or to a more refreshed and lively version of that state you were in before the other word was used by you to induce trance.

When you have left here, you may want to practice and perfect this system of moving through colors, knowing what colors will deepen your trance, and knowing what colors may lighten your trance, experimenting to see if under other conditions, in trance, those colors will have that effect, and doing some work with that color you found to be with you in the most profound depth you were able to achieve.

And I wanted to give you this exercise as a pleasant and restful conclusion to the starting session of the fourth, most demanding cycle of the games.

Each player now will terminate any persisting remnants of trance and you will all go home and further consider what has been said here today.

And you will go knowing that you now have embarked upon the *final* stages of this journey that we, the mind-games players, are all making together.

:: 2 ::

The guide will lead the players through the ASC induction procedure first given in Book One of the games and afterward repeated. In this induction, the players pass through a door, descend a stairway, and arrive at a place where a small boat is waiting. The boat carries the player along through the darkness, and then emerges into sunlight. And the boat continues to float gently downstream, while all of the player's senses are stimulated and brought into play by the suggestions of the guide, the trance thus being deepened.

And, having reached this point in the induction, the guide might say to the players:

Feel yourself going deeper now, as you feel the rocking motion of the boat, to and fro, deeper and deeper, and the sun and the breezes caressing your body.

Hear the lapping of the water now, that soothing sound of the water lapping, and the fish leaping and splashing in the water, and becoming aware now of the birds singing over there along the shore.

Going deeper, and smelling the freshly cut grass over there in the fields, and the flowers blooming along the banks, those smells drifting over to you on the breezes.

You might want to let your arm trail from the boat, so that you feel the cold water on your fingers, and it is very, very clear, clean water, so that you can just bring your fingers up to your lips and have a little taste of that good water, how good and refreshing that water is, as you keep going deeper.

Keep going deeper, and lazily, drowsily, very comfortably continue to drift down and down the stream, and continuing down, continuing down.

And going deeper into trance, until just very easily the boat washes up against the shore, and remaining very, very deeply in trance, and going deeper, get out of the boat, and you will climb on up the bank and find yourself in a meadow where the tall grass is growing, and you can listen to that grass as it seems to whisper, stirring in the breeze. And feeling the grass as it brushes your legs, as you move very lethargically along in that warm sunlight. It is so pleasurable to feel, but it does make you awfully drowsy, does make you very, very drowsy.

And seeing now ahead of you, as you look, a beautiful, big shade tree, a strong, vigorous, but very old tree, and some of its roots are above the ground, and you will notice that there is moss, soft and heavy moss growing on some of those roots. And lying down now, and resting your head on one of the moss-covered roots in the shade, the grass and the ground feeling good to your body, and you find that is an extremely comfortable and pleasurable place to be.

And lying there, aware of everything around you, of the movements of the rabbits out there in the tall grasses, of the squirrels looking down from the branches of the tree, of the wind in the grasses, of the rustling of the leaves, aware of that whole environment and finding it restful, and peaceful, and good.

And feeling yourself to be entirely a part of it, aware of yourself as very much belonging there, and it seems as if you never had any other existence but just being there with the tree and that whole beautiful and harmonious scene.

And feeling yourself so much a part of that scene that you have less and less of a sense of any kind of separateness or singularity, of any apartness, physical or other, from that whole, and losing awareness that there are parts, and aware just of the whole.

And noticing now, and you already knew it, that if you try to find your body, that you really can't tell any more where the back of your head leaves off and the moss-covered roots of that tree begin, or where the roots end and your head begins. Where any of your body leaves off and the earth beneath you begins, or anything about the earth that would allow you to be aware of your body as separate from it, and these notions just drift through awareness, only just barely rippling the surface, because any reference to parts no longer means very much, and there is just a whole.

And the air not differentiated in any way from your body. And noticing it is the same now with sounds, so that you don't know or care any more if any sound is coming from without you or within you, and in fact, within and without are terms that no longer concern you. And whether applied to sight or hearing, or touch or smell, there just really is no within or without, no me and it, no subject, no object, nothing to differentiate anything from anything else.

And no parts, only just a whole, with an increasing awareness of the harmoniousness and beauty of the whole, of being whole, and aware of the wonderful contentment and the joy of this unity, this oneness being experienced so intensely yet quietly by that awareness that is whole.

An awareness that does include relationships, interactions, but is much, much more an awareness of energies, pleasurable energies for the awareness, becoming more intense, more charged, as more and more vitality infuses the whole, with energies more and more intense, more intensely vibrant and energetic, becoming ecstatic for consciousness, moving into a realm where awareness is entirely of blissful sensation, of total, completely fulfilling blissful sensation, that is also emotion, that is also knowing, and that most fundamentally is just pure being.

Ecstatic awareness now of pure being, being ecstatically aware and savoring that awareness of its being, savoring that now, that oneness, that ecstasy, that overwhelming bliss, and completely knowing, and aware, and rapturous in it, for that eternity you will have to experience completely until you are spoken to again. And now forgetting that there is anything else, and much too rapturous to have any awareness that you will be spoken to again, or that there is, or ever was, any you to be spoken to, or that there ever was anything but the whole, the awareness, and the totality of rapture.

The guide will allow the players ample time to have this experience, which can prepare the person for much more profound mind games and experiences to come, and then the guide will say:

You will hear me now, and as you hear me, you will begin to be aware of yourself, and that awareness of your own identity and body will increase. But you will know, having had this experience, about certain possibilities you have, and you will know that you can return to what you now leave behind you.

Leaving that behind you, for what is ahead of you, and finding now that you are aware of your own body in relation to the tree and the ground, and increasingly knowing that you are differentiated from what you see and hear and touch and taste and smell, knowing that your usual mode of functioning is one requiring differentiation, a sense of the withins and withouts, and having a clear sense of being yourself in relation to all of the not-selves experienced by you.

And having a complete sense of your body now, you will

find that the tree and the meadow are losing substance and fade from your awareness. You will remain very deeply in trance, and you will go deeper, and you will know that you are here with me in this place where we are playing the mind games.

We are here together, playing mind games together, learning together to use the mind-body to greater advantage, and learning not just for ourselves, but so that everyone can learn, and know, and experience.

Be aware of that, and go deeper, and in a moment I am going to play some music for you. And with accelerated mental process, AMP as you have learned to let it happen, it will seem to you that several clock-measured minutes of that music will last for an extremely long time, although you will not be concerned with quantities of time. But, if you were, then that music might seem to last for hours, for so long that you would anyway just lose all track of time, knowing only that nothing is happening to interrupt your experiencing of the music, and nothing will interrupt until you have experienced it completely.

On another occasion, you played a game, and your whole body was sensitized to music, so that you heard music as if your entire body was covered with end-organs for hearing, and you also experienced that music as touch sensation, and as colors, and smells, and tastes. That was a very exquisite, aesthetically sensuous, sensual experience of being totally involved with all of your senses in the music.

That is how you are going to hear the music I will play for you, and the intensity of your sensations will just keep building and building, your responses becoming more and more intense, until those combined sensations have become so ecstatically and blissfully intense as to be almost unbearable.

But we will go even one step beyond that, drawing on what you have learned here today, and you will pass on beyond that ecstatic response you are aware of making to the music, going beyond that to lose yourself in the music, and the music will be lost in you. And there will be no you, and no music, but just an experiential oneness, as you have learned how to experience that, and then there will be no limits to the rapturousness, pure experience of pure rapture.

And I am going to play that music for you now.

At the end of these two exercises, which are preparations for "mystical experience," the guide will conduct a gradual re-entry, with suggestions of relaxation preceding those for returning to a refreshed, alert state.

:: 3 ::

The guide will ask the players to self-induce and deepen ASCs and, after that, the guide will give further deepening suggestions. And, after that, the guide will say:

Listen closely now, and be aware just of what is being said. You will remain deeply in trance, and go deeper, and if you are able to be deeply in trance while, at the same time, you are able to open your eyes and to see, then open your eyes now. And if your deep trance requires that your eyes remain closed, then keep your eyes closed, and listen, and go deeper.

And your attention now is being called to the fact that throughout much of history there has been known to occur a very curious experience, curious but of very great power, and countless millions of people still are having that strange and powerful experience today. It is called glossolalia, or speaking in tongues, and people who engage in this practice often have experiences which they describe as being like profound and intense psychedelic drug states, or some of the varieties of religious experiences described by prophets and by saints.

Speaking in tongues was practiced in this country for a long time just by Pentecostals and some other fundamentalist churches, and then it moved into the Episcopal Church, and a few other Protestant churches, and most recently has assumed great importance in some Roman Catholic congregations. And everywhere the experiences are similar, and the context seems to be of minimal importance in shaping the manifestations that occur.

The way this experience is enabled to happen, is that the

minister or guide will place his hands on the forehead of the person, and encourage that person to be open and to allow the Holy Ghost or Holy Spirit to manifest, and that manifestation will use the person's body and there will occur what has been called speaking in tongues.

Strange words or sounds issue from the person's mouth, and some believe that this is an ancient language being spoken, possibly the first fully realized language that was ever spoken on this earth, and the language in which human beings first prayed and otherwise could communicate very directly with God.

Now, listen with great care to what I am saying. Go deeper and deeper, as you listen to what is being said to you. We are going to investigate this experience, and attempt to make it possible, and we will follow the traditional procedure with players who are in a waking state, and with other players who are in trances. And during these experiments, the somnambulists will be given the task of interpreting, if a meaning comes through to them, what is being said by those who are speaking in tongues. And if any other player feels able to function as an interpreter, then that player should request to be heard.

You will take this game very seriously, knowing that we are dealing here with an extremely powerful force that has drastically altered the lives of millions of people, so powerful is it in some of its manifestations. And I will now touch some of you on the shoulder, and those I touch will terminate their trances, so that about half the players will be in trance, and half in their ordinary state of consciousness. Then, we will play this game, as I move from one player to the next, to give each one an opportunity to speak in tongues. And some players without assistance from me will begin to speak in tongues, and this should just be allowed to happen.

But I will pass from one of you to the next, and one by one I will take your foreheads in my hands, and ask you to feel the power manifesting in you, the power that motivates the speaking in tongues. You should open yourself to this power, and allow it to manifest through you, knowing that it is beneficent, so that there is nothing to fear.

I will hold your forehead, and urgently appeal to you to let the force manifest powerfully and with maximum benefit to you, and I will not define the force, although traditionally that force is designated Holy Ghost or Holy Spirit.

Whatever this force may be, let it manifest, and it should not be of any significance what label we attach to it. It may be what is designated by Holy Spirit, it may be some kind of concentrated energy system, or we might regard it as a symbolic manifestation of the God-Idea. But, without attempting to define it, we will exhort it to lay hold of the person receiving the laying on of hands and the urging to have the experience.

The guide will conduct this mind-games session very much in terms of what may result, including the possible use of the interpreters.

At the end of the session, the waking procedure should be carried out as if all of the players are in trance, even though some players were instructed to terminate trance, and no subsequent formal induction was directed at those players.

## :: 4 ::

Players who wish to share trance will arrange themselves in units of a couple or three persons, and these players will induce and deepen one another's trances.

The guide will outline for this game the same procedures followed in previous mind games when trance was shared by couples only.

Players will be given one hour of clock time, with AMP, and urged to endeavor to go deeper and to conduct more profound and far-ranging inner-space explorations than they have done during earlier shared-trance experiences.

The guide will take care to give the usual suggestions preserving the guide's rapport with all players at all times, should it need to be exercised, and will carry out the usual procedures for terminating the shared trances first, then the individual ASCs.

The potentially great importance of these experiences as a

new dimension of human intimacy and interaction on hitherto inaccessible levels should be reaffirmed.

So, too, should be reaffirmed the caution against allowing emotional attachments between the players to develop just on the basis of such little-known interrelationship.

At the conclusion of the hour, the guide and the players, with ASCs terminated, should spend considerable time exploring experiences players have had, and attempting to develop a new knowledge of such experiences.

Players will especially consider possible uses of shared trance in marriage counseling, psychotherapy, and as a means of deepening intimacy between friends, lovers, and possibly other persons with whom it is desirable to reach unusually complete understandings.

:: 5 ::

The guide will say to the players:

We have far to go, and so we will begin.

And now, make use of this well-learned ability you have to go quickly into trance, as your eyes already are closing, closing tight, and you are quickly going deeper, deeper, and deeper, into trance.

And I'm going now to give you two minutes of clock time, and during that time, when I tell you to start, you will experience yourself as floating down, then as drifting down, as the trance keeps deepening, and then falling, faster and faster, down through dark, seemingly infinite spaces, falling farther and farther and having sensations of falling that will carry you very, very deeply into trance. And you have all that time, beginning *now!*

The guide next will say:

And now, you will find that you are falling, but falling more slowly, and still more slowly, as you near the most profound depths, within this *circular* space where you are going to settle softly, easily, down upon a substance able to support you here in the *cylindrical* depths of your trance.

You are going to learn important things here, and it is likely that you will have experiences both powerful and beautiful. At the same time, you will be preparing yourself for even more ultimate ones, as you go deeper now, and even deeper, and deeper into this altered state necessary for the experiences you will have.

And you will now find yourself becoming aware, gradually at first, of rays of white light reaching down to you, sparkling white light, a cone of that light, surrounding you now, growing brighter and brighter, sparkling and shimmering, warming you with its radiance. As it washes over you, suffusing your whole body, changing in appearance from one moment to the next, but always brilliantly white, cascading around you and sometimes appearing to you now as a white and golden light.

A wondrously beautiful white and golden light, dazzling, unearthly, all around you as your body moves into it, feeling your body beginning to merge with it, and feeling your body becoming much taller, and a feeling of more and more elongation, the body becoming taller, slimmer, and this bringing with it what you are experiencing now as an indescribable but strongly spiritual feeling, something more than human that your body is feeling as you stand there so tall, elongated, with the dazzling white and golden light all around you, and so much a part of you that your body now seems to you more a body of light than of flesh.

And that light continues glowing brighter and brighter, as you feel yourself to be merging with the light, becoming the light, and finding your awareness now to be of yourself as a shower of sparks descending, descending to become a pool of white light, there on the ground, where your awareness is, where you are, and you *are* a pool of white light, pool of energies, about to be unleashed.

Energies, forces gathering there, and that white light now leaping upward, soaring upward, a column of white and golden fire, reaching up and up and up, through that almost endlessly long cylindrical space, a column of white and golden flame that you are a part of, and you have no awareness beyond the column of white and golden fire.

A column that is glowing whiter and whiter, a column of white fire that you are a part of, reaching upward from the very center of the earth, surging, flowing upward and upward, and finally bursting out through the opening at the earth's surface, and still surging upward, far, far up into the skies.

A pillar of white light, rising from the earth's center, and soaring outward endlessly into the black vastnesses of space, as if its power would allow it to penetrate the universe. And knowing the feeling of awesome power, of sublime beauty, and wonder, and energy, as you partake of that great column of white fire.

But feeling yourself now sinking backward with it, back and down again, back past the earth's surface, down and down the cylinder, until down at the bottom only a small white flame is burning. And you arise out of that fire, and the fire is extinguished.

And becoming aware of your body of flesh, but changed, and as if your body has passed through some kind of important catharsis of fire, as if your body has been made new by that experience, as if you have been given access to more vital energies and powers than your body could draw upon before.

Going deeper and deeper, and able to go deeper and deeper, and finding yourself here in this place with me, but having access to some very potent energies within you. And focus your consciousness now on the base of your spine, wholly focused on the base of your spine, becoming aware of a pool of gently swirling but potentially extremely powerful energies there.

Focus on that pool, and, at first slowly, notice that you can experience a tingling, and then increasingly stronger sensations, as you direct that energy to rise along your spine. And be aware now of its power growing, and growing, and feel it as it gains momentum, slowly, as it gains more force, as it rises.

And know that it has the capacity to surge with enormous force all the way up to your brain, triggering a kind of explosion of energy there, and that this could trigger an activation of more and more brain cells, and powerful electrical and chemical reactions, events in your brain that could very greatly change you, giving you access to powers presently only latent within you.

Be conscious again now of that energy system slowly rising up along your spine, restraining it in order that it can accumulate force enough, but not preventing its movement, holding that movement to a slow, steady progress, up your spine, and observing it closely, estimating when the tension is sufficient to effect a surging up into your brain, but not with such great force as to be overwhelming, and you will have a reliable sense of how much force you can contain.

You will know when to stop holding back, and when you do release that tensed power, then it will erupt and surge upward to your brain, and if the force released is powerful enough, then it will trigger that explosion in your brain, and that liberation of powers that I have described to you.

And now, concentrate on the task of directing those energies up and along through your spine, directing them upward until you feel the accumulation of tensions, and until you feel that by letting go, you can send those energies surging to your brain. And then let go.

The guide will allow the players ample time to endeavor to carry out the instructions, but will be prepared to learn that only partial successes were achieved in the raising of this energy. And should an occasional player be successful, that player will be someone who by various means has become prepared for such success, and will be able to experience the phenomenon with safety and, probably, benefit.

But most players, and more likely all players, will not complete the exercise, and the guide should congratulate these players on the measure of success they did have. The players should be told to remember in detail how they became aware of the energy, and how they managed to achieve such success as they did achieve in causing it to rise. The players will be told that success is possible, but usually only with considerable practice. However, an unusually good beginning has been made.

ASCs will be terminated, and the players will discuss both experiences they have had.

## :: 6 ::

The players by prearrangement will meet before departing for an experience of prolonged fasting, isolation, and meditation.

Deep trances will be induced and the guide then will speak to the players, instructing them:

During the forty-eight hours of isolation demanded by this mind game, you will not eat at all and you only will drink just as much as is necessary so that thirst will not distract you.

And you will meditate, while deeply in trance, on a few very fundamental questions.

You will remember that God has spoken always to human beings in dreams and visions, and that rarely have there ever been reports of exceptions to this historical fact. And you will meditate deeply on why this is so, and you will consider implications, and go into this matter thoroughly, meditating with words and with images and possibly utilizing other approaches, and this might include prayer.

And you will meditate upon the question: What is ultimate reality? And what do I mean and understand by a term such as "ultimate reality," and what could anyone mean by that? And how might that reality be known?

Considering this question, you will try by various means to explore whether the way to awareness of an ultimate reality is to go deeper and deeper into more profoundly altered states of awareness, reaching a depth at which awareness expands greatly outward, and without loss of profundity. And if you reach that point, and continue with that expansion, is there a point necessarily arrived at where or when all awareness of self is lost, so that in some sense you cease to be? And should you reach that point of ceasing to be, and then return later back to self-awareness, how might you be able to know what, if anything, happened to that self while it was not aware of itself, and if it is affirmed that the self while not aware of itself was united with God or with an ultimate reality, what could be the basis for such a claim?

And you will not just explore these matters by thinking about them, but you will try to explore them experientially and directly, by moving as far as you can in the direction of deepening, expansion, and the plunging of the self into the unknown.

Go deeper, and know that in these meditations, you will be especially aided by certain experiences you have had while playing the mind games, and in particular some of the fourth-cycle games. All of the experiences of all of the mind games will be of benefit in your endeavors, but especially some of the games we have played since we began the fourth cycle, and your unconscious mind will know how to make the best use of these recent gains.

You will meditate on the fundamental questions mentioned, and on reality just in its relationship to human consciousness, and if you find yourself deviating from these meditations, you will practice the deepening of your altered state. And you will sleep just as little as possible, utilizing AMP with suggestions that a few minutes of sleep will be sufficient, as you did on the previous occasion of isolation and fasting.

To avoid misunderstanding, let it be stated that these meditations do not impose any kind of belief on anyone. You will begin, for example, with your own notions about what is meant by God, and about what others have meant by God, and in the course of the meditations, your beliefs may or may not be significantly altered by what you will experience.

What you are being instructed to do, is to limit yourself to prolonged consideration, by a variety of means, of a limited number of questions which are, however, questions of great scope and depth. You must make every effort to stay with these questions, and success in that endeavor assuredly will lead you into experiences such as you are not likely to have had before.

At the end of the forty-eight hours, without speaking to anyone, insofar as that is possible, you will return here and this group of players will reconvene to examine the experiences the players respectively have had.

The guide will then terminate the altered states, and request the players to go without any conversation or delay to the place each player has chosen to carry out the fast and solitary meditation exercises.

:: 7 ::

This game must be played in a secluded and pleasant natural setting, and in comfortable weather. If these specifications cannot be met, then this game should be omitted from the cycle, and the players will proceed on to the next game. However, it will be worth considerable effort to arrange for the necessary site.

The players having assembled in this natural setting, the guide will request that the players self-induce ASCs and then deepen those states as profoundly as possible. When, individually, the deepest possible states have been reached, then a player will become aware of this and will communicate it to the guide by the head involuntarily falling forward. The head will slowly fall forward, and will remain fallen forward for about a minute, and then involuntarily raise back up again.

When this has been done, the guide will say:

Remaining deeply now in trance, in a moment I am going to ask you to open your eyes, and to stand, and you will move about, remaining in trance, and going deeper and deeper, as I continue to speak to you and as you continue to respond very well to the suggestions that will be offered to you.

Should any player feel that she or he is unable to maintain a trance with the eyes opened, that player will open eyes anyway, and move around with the rest of the players, while *vividly imagining* how those suggestions would be responded to if that player were in trance. That player will behave as if in a deep trance, and it is very probable that later the player who began by vividly imagining that she or he was in deep trance and responding, will discover that it is no longer required to imagine a trance, because at some point the trance has become a reality, and the person will have been in trance for an indeterminate period. The player will discover the fact of the trance in the course of effortlessly and effectively responding to some suggestion. And the player thereafter will be able to go readily into these deep trances and maintain them while moving about and performing all sorts of functions.

And now you will go deeper, and you *will* open your eyes, and look up, first of all, at the sky. And look at the sky as if you were seeing that sky at the very dawn of creation, as if it were something being perceived by human eyes for the first time.

*Everything* in this environment is going to be sensed in a novel way, everything as if completely new to you, and also as if your activity in using your senses in the ways you will use them is something that is novel for you.

And you are becoming aware of great changes in the reality you are perceiving, and noticing now that this place where we are seems to be out of time, to be an *eternal, timeless, mythic*, and even *sacred* space.

Look, and all around you are animate and inanimate forms having characteristics of singularity, originality—as if each were the very first of its kind to appear on this earth. As if these things were God's prototypes, or first creations of what each one is.

And this feeling grows, that we are dwelling here in a kind of mythic realm, and that feeling intensifies, as you look about you at the trees. Look at them, closely, and note the incredible intricacy of the patterning of the leaves of those trees, and the artistry manifest in the way the branches and the leaves coexist as parts, each one complete in itself, but also harmoniously integrated and orchestrated into that very complex and beautiful whole.

Look at the bark of the tree—the images, the worlds, that

emerge from that bark—and touch it, knowing it by means of touching it, with your eyes opened and with your eyes closed, and smell it, and now put your ear against the bark, and listen.

And you're going to wander around for a while, touching the earth and the grass, lying down sometimes to look upward at trees and sky, having a tactile awareness even of the air around you as you pass through it, or as you experience it when you are unmoving.

And you will have five minutes as measured by the clock, but it will seem to you that you have hours, or however long you might want, to move around and savor the full beauty and uniqueness of this wonderful place. At the end of that time, when we gather here together again, I would like to communicate further with you. Now go, and explore, and enjoy the wealth of experience that awaits you.

When the players have returned, the guide will say:

Now just keep going deeper and deeper, going even deeper now, and savoring the harmony of this place, becoming aware of it as a place of extraordinary serenity, letting the serenity permeate your being, taking root throughout your body-mind, so that you can call it forth again, so that it always will be there for you.

And now, become aware of the joy of this place, experience the joy that is all around you, the joy that is also arising within you, and becoming stronger, learning that joy as it becomes an essential part of you, so that you can call it forth again.

And please listen to me now with total concentration, listening intently, completely concentrated on learning and assimilating what is going to be said to you now.

Please become aware of the ground, feel the ground beneath your feet. Stand there lifting first one foot and next the other foot, and then firmly plant both of your feet upon the earth. And feel now through the bottoms of your feet, roots that go down, roots going down and down and down, and know that these are symbolic roots. They will not immobilize you or fetter you in any way, but you will receive a kind of nourishment through them.

And you will know that these symbolic roots do stand for something that is very real. You will know that what you are experiencing here is an authentic restoration, and that the symbolic does have reality, and great power. Authentic restoration, your roots, your rootedness in nature, that nature of which you always were a part, and from which you have become somewhat detached and alienated as you supposed you were separate from it. But now you know that you are not separate from it, that you are an individual and free, but also that you are a part of this whole, and that you can experience yourself and nature as part of a harmony in which you share, so that you feel now completely at home in this world.

And it will be as if, having gone away for a while, you have come back home, to your roots, to the sources of your life and of your strength. You will not lose again your awareness of wholeness, and you will not lose the capacity to partake of the nourishment that nature offers to you. And nature sustains and provides for every being that is a part of this creation. Just be aware of that for a while now, and let that realization flood you and fill you. And be aware only of these matters of which I have just spoken to you, until I address you once again.

The guide, observing the players, will decide when to go on to the next stage of the game, and when it *is* decided to go on, the guide will say to the players:

Remain deeply in your altered state of awareness, and go still deeper and continue going deeper, as you spend the next hour or two in profound appreciation of all that is around you. During that time you will wander through this place, and we will eat the food we have brought here with us, and we will drink the water and milk we have brought. We will savor these simple foods and drinks, taking a very great pleasure in them, and feeling yourself, your body, to be richly nourished by this food and drink. And you will not exchange words with one another, but may communicate in any other way, silently appreciating other players as you appreciate and know the sky, trees, birds, animals—everything that is here in this place.

And as you do this, your consciousness will alter more and more profoundly, and your awareness will expand so that you will be aware in the usual ways of the objects perceived by your senses, but also aware of those perceived objects much more acutely, and as having many kinds of realities, as expressions of nature's artistry, as creations of God, as having meanings never thought of by you before, never apprehended before. So that you will be aware of your world and your perceptions in many, many ways. And those awarenesses will not be products of an effort to think or perceive in novel ways, but they will just come to you, just appear to you. And you may not have the awarenesses I have suggested to you, but something entirely different, awarenesses expressive of your own experience, of your own surfaces and depths, and in no sense shaped by what has been said to you.

You will have a great deal of time for this experience, and when that very long time has elapsed, I will summon the players by the tinkling of a bell, and you will return. And, for the purposes of your playing of this game, you will have all the space you could possibly require within a radius of about one hundred yards, as I stand here at the center. Please go now, and begin.

When the players have been summoned to return, the guide will speak to them, saying:

Very soon the night is going to fall. We will build our fire now, and spread our blankets in preparation for spending the night here in this place. You will spend about the next thirty minutes making those preparations, and during that time you may terminate ASCs, move up to a somewhat lighter level, remain as you are, or you might want to go deeper. But if you would like a change and perhaps some time spent in your ordinary state, please do that now.

When the players have brought the logs and the kindling, arranged their blankets, and completed other preparations, the guide will ascertain that the blankets are arranged in a circle and at a comfortable distance from the place where the fire will be, and then will say:

Now, if you did terminate or lighten your trance, please go back into a state about as deep as any you have reached here today, and you will find that you can rather quickly do that, and please do it now.

And you may want to go deeper, and you can continue doing that as I speak, as I ask that you make yourself very comfortable there, and you will be asked in a moment to perform a task that can be of great importance and value for you.

What you must do now is meditate upon the forty-eight hours of fasting, isolation, and very rich experiences undergone by you recently. Go over what happened during that time, and the conversations we later had about it, and the thinking about it you have done since then, and you will integrate all of that, and you also will bring it together with everything experienced by you here today. And you will let all of this flow together, until it becomes one integrated whole, and I will allow you fifteen or twenty minutes for this, and your mind will accelerate sufficiently so that it all can be accomplished with that amount of clock time, and now you will begin.

Later on, the fire will be lighted, the players will observe the fire, and the guide will say to them:

Going deeper and deeper as you look into the fire, deeper and looking and looking at the fire, perceiving images there, and you will find yourself traveling back in time, back in time, and back to an occasion when the earliest people sat together by a fire, and you are feeling something of what they felt, and responding to the fire as they responded. And you really can feel that now, and you do feel it.

But your mental processes accelerating now, and you will have five minutes of clock time to move back up across the millennia, from the time of those earliest people, moving up through the centuries, experiencing *everything* that *fire* has meant to mankind, as a tool, as a scourge, as a symbol, all of those relationships human beings have had with fire, the human meaning of fire, and experience that beginning *now!*

The guide will give similar instructions to the players with respect to experiencing earth, and air, and water, all with AMP, each within five minutes of clock-measured time.

And next, the guide will urge to the players to go deeper, and still deeper, and will designate one of the players to perform the function of priestess, and in that role to invoke the spirit of the moon.

The players will observe the moon, and the priestess will describe the beauty of the moon, and what it has meant to mankind. She will call upon the moon as a symbolic force, for so long an object of worship, to which so many great powers have been attributed, expressing the wish that the moon will shine down protectively upon the planet earth.

And the priestess will call upon the moon especially to watch over, and protect, and inspire the gathering of the mind-games players.

The guide then will designate a second player to call upon the group to observe with him or her the beauty of the night sky, and of the stars.

And this player will make a brief address to the heavens, describing what the stars have meant to mankind, illumining the night, and the powers that people always have supposed to reside in the heavens. Recalling that the gods have so often been said to dwell there, and calling upon whatever intelligent life of any kind might reside anywhere in the cosmos, to receive from the players expressions of love and good will, and calling upon all life to return this expression.

The guide will then say to the players:

And now, sit for just a little longer, looking again intently at the fire, and becoming, as you look at the fire, more and more drowsy, becoming extremely sleepy. And soon you are going to feel just as if you have been given an extremely potent beverage, to send you off to sleep, a powerful sleeping draught, and the sleep you will sleep will be most profound.

And during that sleep, there will arise within you images representing forces within you that are forces to heal you, to give you energy and strength, serenity, confidence, forces to move you toward the achieving of your most important goals. You are almost asleep now, and you can barely stay awake long enough for me to say to you that you will awaken at dawn, and soon after that we will leave here, and now you do fall into that deep sleep.

Next morning, the players will be greeted by the guide, and instructed to quietly observe the dawn, to savor feelings of refreshment, renewal, and to become increasingly alert, energetic, and to feel as wide awake as the player ever has felt, and even more wide awake than that!

Players then will be told to remove all traces of their having been in that place, and, after that, without lingering to talk, to go their respective ways.

:: 8 ::

ASCs will be induced and deepened, by the players or by the guide, and players will be told that involuntary left arm levitations will inform both player and guide that a player has reached the deepest ASC level that can presently be reached.

When all players have offered this signal, or, if not, have been verbally responsive to the guide, then the guide will say:

You are going to pass through a series of experiences utilizing your ability to accelerate mental processes, so that very great amounts of subjective experience are able to occur within very small amounts of clock-measured time. You have, of course, utilized this AMP frequently, but some especially important demands will be made of that capacity today.

First of all, now, you are going to have an experience that will be very pleasurable for you and, if you do really respond, will probably exceed all of your expectations about how pleasurable this experience is going to be. And it also will take you deeper, much deeper, and I want to tell you something more about the experience before you will have it, when receiving the instruction to begin.

And, when you do receive that instruction, you will begin to experience, with images, sensory stimulation to which you will find yourself responding with great intensity and sensory pleasure. You will experience with all of your senses, and what you experience will be provided by your own unconscious mind, drawing upon the knowledge of what kind of sensory stimuli you will respond to with the greatest intensity and pleasure.

There will be a great variety of stimuli that you are going to experience, so that you are going to be stimulated in a great variety of ways. And there can be an enormous diversity of settings, and objects, and people, and whatever is especially gratifying to you, and these pleasure experiences will reinforce one another, and accumulate, so that your pleasure will keep on building into a powerful concentration of multisensory stimulation that will surpass what is usually described by people as pleasure, and move on into realms more likely to be described as bliss, rapture, and ecstasy.

These pleasures can be aesthetic, erotic, every and any kind of sensuous, sensual stimulation and gratification, until your body has been stimulated to the point of sensory overloading, stimulated beyond all previous experiential boundaries, and you will experience all that you can endure and still know to be pleasure. And for this, you will utilize AMP, and you will have five minutes of clock time, and that will be time enough for you to experience a seemingly endless amount of stimulation, to experience endless pleasure, exquisite, ecstatic, and you will begin to receive those images of sensory stimulation starting *now!*

At the end of the allotted time, the guide will again address the players:

Whatever your experience just now may have been, whatever the extent to which you responded, you will feel yourself going deeper, going deeper and deeper, and far away from the surface, far away from the sensory world, and when I tell you to start you will have five minutes of clock-measured time and during that time you will find yourself observing or even participating in the significant events of your life as you have lived it right up until the present moment.

You will encounter all the people who have had important meanings for you. You will find recurring important events that have shaped you, and you will understand, in some cases for the first time, the true nature of your relationships with those persons, and the real way in which those significant events of your life contributed to the formation of that person you now are. It may seem to you that you are reliving large segments of your life, but that you are able to revise your interpretations and understandings of various events as they recur. And it may be you will re-experience something that happened to you when you were a child, and that you then misunderstood and allowed to be detrimental to you, and you may still be suffering from the consequences of that childish misunderstanding. But now, from the vantage point of greater maturity, when you re-experience that event, you will be able to correct the misinterpretation that you made before, and alter that event's impact upon both your conscious and unconscious mind, so that the past error no longer can affect your behavior or affect you in any way at all.

You are going to have this very concentrated re-experiencing of the significant events of your life, and there will be all the time you need for this, and you will begin right *now!*

At the end of the allotted five minutes, the guide will say:

And now, you will find yourself going deeper, and setting aside for the moment all that you have just experienced, and for now you will not give any further thought to what has just happened to you. Nothing will be forgotten, but for now your awareness will be completely filled by the words being spoken to you, and you will go deeper.

Going deeper and deeper now, and allowing much deeper processes and contents of your mind to manifest to you. I am going to give you five minutes of clock time, with AMP, and that will be all the time you will need to have the very rich experience you are going to have, and will have in a little while, when you are instructed to begin.

But first, as you keep going deeper, I do want to suggest to you that what you experienced during the preceding segment of this game may now be translated by your unconscious mind into symbols and symbolic dramas, and you may find a drama taking the form of a legend or a myth. It will certainly be some kind of dramatic sequence, and it will be a symbolic expression of you and your life, and it may result in giving you valuable insights, and some very serious problems could be resolved in the course of this experiencing by you of your own theater of symbols, this theater of your own deep psyche, and you may be carried forward to growth and understanding and a state of health representing considerable advances for you.

Your unconscious mind understands very well what I have said and what is to be done, and you will have that experience starting *now!*

At the end of this period, the guide will say to the players:

Go deeper, and what you just experienced will not concern your conscious mind now, but all that you have experienced here today will contribute importantly to what is next in store for you, as you move into the final and most profound stage of this mind game.

There remains this fourth, much deeper and final level of experience for you to have, and you will go deeper now into trance, and let yourself now go very deep, and listen to what will be said to you before you are told to move into that fourth and final level.

In a little while, you are going to penetrate far beyond the images of your own life, and beyond all symbols that are personal for you, going deeper and deeper into realms of awareness no longer recognizable as having any relation to your personal life, no longer recognizable as in any way expressions of your self.

And these are realms that may seem to be transpersonal, part of the collective experience of a whole culture or people, possibly even of all mankind. And passing through the antipodes of the mind, through realms of archetypes and universal symbols that may seem to have their own independent reality, their own actual existence.

And you will keep on going deeper, deeper into trance and penetrating deeper, knowing primordial reservoirs of energy out of which these images rise, perhaps out of which all objects rise, places of primeval power that nourishes creation.

And you may find yourself still going deeper, or you may experience your movement as a surging upward, into realms that are sometimes called superconscious, where become possible awarenesses that are at once the highest and the most profound, most expanded of which any human being is capable. You will move toward that realm of experience, and if you are able to go far enough, you will have some kind of experience of ultimate reality, Ground of Being, primordial energy, whatever your own experience may be, should you be able to go that far.

You will have the same five minutes of clock time, but that will be irrelevant should you penetrate into dimensions where time does not seem to exist, and one simply knows that that realm is beyond our space-time, and is eternal.

You will go now as deep and as far as you can, and you will begin that movement *now!*

At the end of the time allotted, the guide will closely observe the individual players, taking care not to disturb any player who seems not to have completed whatever is being experienced, but suggesting to other players that ASCs now be terminated, and the player return to an alert, waking state.

Subsequent to this final segment of the game, the guide will arrange the players in small groups of two or three or four persons, known by the guide to be especially close to one another. And these players then will discuss together what has occurred, and whatever a player wishes to discuss in relation to this game.

After that, if a player's experience warrants, the guide will suggest to the player a silent period during which there will occur an integration of what has been experienced.

And each player will be told to return to her or his home when fully ready to depart.

## :: 9 ::

Players will be asked by the guide to induce and deepen ASCs, and to take about ten minutes to do this, after which more instructions will be given.

Players then will be told that they are going, once again, to evoke the Group Spirit, called up in earlier cycles of the games, but this time giving to it an even greater measure of energy, consciousness, a kind of real existence, and the players will firmly believe for the duration of the game that they are able to do this, and that they have done it.

The guide will say to the players:

Go deeper, and just for the duration of this game, you are being programed with a belief-system to the effect that the Group Spirit has become an actual, intelligent being, conscious, and powerful, although limited by the conditions to be set forth. And the belief-system regulating your understanding of the Group Spirit will continue until I or someone else assuming my guiding function brings the mind game to termination.

The guide then will tell the players to open their eyes without any concern for the state of consciousness they will be in when they do so, and that whatever state it may be is acceptable, and the players should pay close attention to the guide, who next will say:

We are beginning to go now into trance together. We are going to experience deepening together, and, finally, each of us will contribute to the pool of consciousness out of which the Group Spirit will draw its substance and arise to exist once again.

And now we will breathe rhythmically together, gradually bringing our breathing together, until we are all exhaling and inhaling in perfect unison, and we will continue to do that for a while, and then I will speak to you again. And let us begin that breathing now, and as we breathe we are creating our unity of consciousness.

Next, the guide will say to the players:

And now, we are going to chant together. We will chant the OM together, beginning when I indicate the beginning by raising up my hand, and ending when I indicate the ending by raising my hand for the second time. And, as we chant together, going into an altered state of consciousness together, and going deeper.

After this, the guide will urge the players to keep going deeper together, and will lead the players as together they repeat after the guide:

> And we now are becoming,
> and all of us are becoming,
> all of us becoming one mind.
> One mind, one mind, one mind.
> One mind, one mind, one mind.
> One trance, one trance, one trance.
> One trance, one trance, one trance.
> One ever-deepening trance.

One ever-deepening trance.
One ever-deepening trance.
One mind, one trance, one mind, one trance,
one trance, one ever-deepening trance,
one trance, one ever-deepening trance.

The guide will continue repeating these lines for as long as it seems appropriate to do so, and then will say:

Now, give me the whole of your attention, and know that you are sharing in this trance we all share, and that you are this trance which we all are.

And we are gathered here in this circle, so that now you will look at the center of the circle, and from each of us is flowing into that center streams of consciousness, streams of energy, streams of light, creating a pool of consciousness there, a pool to which we are all contributors, a pool partaking of the whole of what we are, so that the pool of consciousness is far greater in its potential than any one of us. And not just as great as all our capacities combined, but much greater than that, and as powerful as one entity would be if all of these capacities could be combined in just one being.

And we are going to cause to rise now, out of that pool, the entity we have called the Group Spirit.

Those who are able to maintain a deep trance with eyes opened, now will open their eyes, so as to witness the emergence of the Group Spirit. And other players will become aware in other ways of the coming of the presence we are calling up.

You will be aware of that emergence, and of the Group Spirit's location in space, there at the center. And you will concentrate on that space, focus intensely and remain focused on that space, and understand now we can and must *materialize* the Group Spirit, endowing that entity with a sufficiently material being that it can appear to us all. And more, if we are successful enough, we will be able to apprehend the Group Spirit with any one of our senses—be able to see it, and hear it, and we even could touch it, were it not necessary to take certain precautions, which will be taken. But we

200

*can* materialize this entity, by concentrating on the center and vividly imagining, powerfully imagining, the flow of substance, of material, from you and into that center, where the pool has been created by us.

The image of matter, the image of substance, flowing from us to the center, and the image will materialize as the substance of the Group Spirit.

Concentrate on this task to the exclusion of all else, and with total dedication, and you will continue with that until I say to you the single word *stop!*

After instructing the players to stop, the guide will ascertain how many of the players now are aware of the Group Spirit, and in what ways.

If the presence of the Group Spirit is not definitely known by at least two of the players, then the process of pouring consciousness and power into the pool will be repeated, and then the materialization process, until some or all players experience the presence.

When the players do perceive the Group Spirit, then the guide will advance to the center, and inside the circle made by the players, the guide will inscribe a smaller circle, which will be defined by the guide as surrounding the pool of consciousness out of which the Group Spirit was born. And the guide next will say:

We do contain now this Group Spirit within the circle that I have created by moving to encircle that Group Spirit three times. And, from this moment, it may remain there, within our awareness, existing now independently of us, for so long as we do not withdraw from the pool the consciousness and power this entity requires to be able to survive.

We have gathered here to raise up this Group Spirit, embodiment of us all and of our work together.

We have raised it to celebrate our joint achievements, all that we have experienced together, and to celebrate the unity of purpose and experience we bring to the work we still must do.

We will celebrate these things in the form of the Group Spirit, and we will open ourselves to that spirit one by one, allowing that spirit to inspire us with the means by which each of us may celebrate it best.

The guide will then designate a player, and say to her:

You are the first to be chosen. Arise now. Go and stand before the place we have designated to be the residing place of this entity we have evoked. Request inspiration in the form of a dance or a song or a chant, something that can be performed by you now, as an offering and in celebration of the spirit of our group.

After that, as instructed by the guide, each player successively will stand near the center of the circle, receiving inspiration, and then carrying out whatever movements or sounds or other behavior the person feels motivated to do and experiencing this motivation as coming directly from the Group Spirit.

When every player has celebrated the Group Spirit, then the guide will say:

Go deeper now, and make yourself comfortable, and in just a very short while, you are going to fall asleep. You are becoming quite drowsy already, and you will fall into a deep, deep sleep, and that sleep will last for about thirty minutes of clock-measured time. But you will not go to sleep until these instructions are completed, and you know what is to be done.

And during that sleep, you will be moving quickly down to a level at which you are vividly dreaming. The Group Spirit will appear to you in a dream, and you will be able to gain a clear and detailed impression of its appearance, and you may be able to enter into a conversation with it, and various things might be revealed to you. You will remember your entire dream, and at the end of the thirty minutes, you will remain in trance but will waken from your sleep, and then in your notebook you will make a sketch and notes concerning the dream manifestion of the Group Spirit. And these materials will allow you to make a more detailed drawing or painting and more complete notes later on.

After you have recorded your dream, you will also quickly sketch the Group Spirit as you were aware of it previous to your dream, and also as you are aware of it at the time of your sketching, and augment these with written notes. These, too, can be much amplified by you at a future time. And now, you are so sleepy that you are unable to remain awake any longer, but you are deeply impressed with the instructions given you, and now do go to sleep.

When the players have wakened and completed their sketches and notes, the guide will inquire if any player feels herself or himself to be in unusually close rapport with the Group Spirit, and if any player feels this, then efforts will be made to establish good communication and to ask questions and receive answers from the entity. The guide will encourage communication with the entity for as long as this seems productive, and then will say:

Please be silent now, and go deeper, and be aware of nothing but the words spoken to you. The instructions you are going to receive are of great importance, and you must give your whole attention to what you will have to do, and you will do it correctly.

And now, for what may be the last time, we will let go of this Group Spirit to which we have given birth and nourishment and substance. We will let go of it, and when we do let go, then it will in no sense exist any more as an entity with an independent existence of its own. It will exist only as a memory, and we will remember what we have learned by, temporarily, calling up something that did seem to exist apart from us, and in a way that made it unlike any other existence within our experience.

We are going to remember the spirit of this group, and the symbolic form that expressed it, and we are going to remember what we have learned about modifications of reality that may occur and be shared when a collective consciousness accidentally or by intention comes into being. And we will remember that a collective consciousness may create something that greatly exceeds in power the sum of the contributing, individual minds.

We will reflect on these matters and their meaning for religion, for politics, for war, and for peace, and for the shaping of reality and human experience generally. And we will comprehend more and more about the meaning of this experience as time goes by.

And direct your awareness now toward that symbolic thought form, that Group Spirit, and withdraw from the pool along the same lines that you fed into it, withdrawing the consciousness, the energy, the life-force, the power that you fed into that pool, and that you fed into the Group Spirit.

Withdraw, pull back to yourself, the image of matter, the image of substance, those vivid images transmitted by you for the purpose of materializing the Group Spirit, and now have vivid images of that matter and substance all returning back to you.

As you do these things, you will be aware that the Group Spirit as a symbolic form becomes less and less of a reality, that its being is becoming very pale and thin, and that it is passing out of existence as the pool ceases to exist, as each of you absorbs back into yourself that which you relinquished for a while.

You will also be aware that you are stronger, more knowledgeable; that you as an individual have been enriched because of your participation in that pooling of consciousness; that you have brought something back from that pool, and this enrichment will stay with you.

In just a moment, this game will be concluded, and with it, of course, the belief-system programed in with respect to the Group Spirit. And also, as this mind game ends, players are not in any way collectivized or merged. The egos are quite distinct. Each of you is quite separate from any other person, a separate person, a well-defined individual, and becoming even more completely yourself as you realize yourself more completely in the liberation of potentials resulting from the playing of the games.

Finally, now, there are a few more instructions that have to be given you. Before we next meet, you will complete the drawings or paintings, perhaps even sculptures—those works of art representing in a literal way the Group Spirit as you experienced it.

You will remember those dances or songs or other performances you gave in celebrating the Group Spirit. And quite likely, when you repeat those performances, you will discover that they are means by which you can go very quickly into ASCs, and means you can utilize to effect deepening. Other players may be similarly affected by your celebration performance, and you by theirs.

When we meet again, but not before, we will compare the works of art the players have created as literal representations of the Group Spirit. Then we will have some indication as to how similar or different our experiences were.

The guide will then repeat that the belief-system will be terminated with the trances, and will restore the players to an alert, refreshed waking state.

:: *10* ::

The players will bring with them their works of art representing the Group Spirit, and will have been instructed by the guide to have coverings over those works, so that they will not be seen accidentally by other players.

On arrival, the players will be asked to keep the works covered, and to lay them aside until later, when all work will be looked at by all of the players.

ASCs will be induced and deepened, and the guide will say:

We will now create together an abstract work of art to which each player will successively contribute, as we have worked together in the past, and we will continue working until we know that we have finished.

This work of art will be a collective expression of the total experience of the Group Spirit, as we all had that experience during the last game.

We will not perform any action to renew the existence of the Group Spirit, but our expression will be in the nature of a memory of something that existed in the past, but is no more and will not be again.

We will feel great unity and harmony as we execute this work.

Each one of us will feel that the artist-capacity of the person is dominant for consciousness, and will do work that is the expression of that artist consciousness each of us has.

And I will make the first mark on the canvas, and then designate, one by one, which player is to go next, until every player has made some contribution.

When players feel that the work is completed, they will take seats, and when three-quarters of the players are seated, the guide will then determine when to declare the work finished, and will say to the players: "It is done."

After this determination by the guide, the ASCs will be terminated, and the players will examine and discuss both the work just completed and the individual works from the previous session.

By this and other means the players will attempt to arrive at agreement concerning the meaning of the Group Spirit, and will explore the significance of this meaning for the group and for the games remaining.

:: 11 ::

Players will be told they are going to play another shared-trance game and those who wish to participate should group themselves in couples. These players should seat themselves facing one another, and at a distance from players who have decided to be observers only.

When this has been done, the guide will inquire if any other players would like to choose partners for this game before it begins. The guide will add that this time specific joint explorations will be suggested, and that some especially rich experiences may be in the offing. Players who wish to change their minds and choose partners for this game, now have their last opportunity to do so.

After this, the guide will instruct the observers to remain silent throughout the game, and will speak to the participating players:

First of all, I am going to give you instructions, or describe to you possibilities, which you might want to explore and realize in your shared trance. But before that is done, I would like to request you to now self-induce ASCs, and to go as deep as you possibly can during the next several minutes before I speak to you again. And please begin that induction and deepening now.

Next the guide will say:

And now go still deeper, deeper and deeper into trance, aware only of what I am saying to you. Your body is very relaxed and comfortable, so that you don't even have to be aware of your body, just aware of what is being said, and totally concentrated on what is being said. And with every word and image you receive, you will continue to go deeper and deeper into trance.

Later, when you will share trance with your partner, your covoyager on a profound journey you will make, you and that companion will have some important tasks to perform— tasks that are of great importance for you, and tasks that you may be able to carry out to the benefit of all of us.

And you, later on with your partner, will venture into other realities, mythic realities, legendary realities, or whatever those realities might turn out to be. Sometimes going very far back through time together, or taking whatever path you may discover that will best enable you to arrive at your goal.

You are going to have the task, first of all, of trying to find the answer or some knowledge about an important secret or mystery concerning which people have been seeking answers for hundreds and, in some cases, thousands of years. And I will suggest to you that you may be pursuing knowledge of one of the following mysteries or objects or events.

One of these could be the Holy Grail, and the grail, as you know, is the chalice from which Christ is said to have drunk at the Last Supper.

And later it was taken to the place where Christ was crucified, and some of the blood of the crucified Christ was collected in that chalice. And the chalice became an object of very great power and sanctity. According to legend, it would be found from time to time, and then great miracles would be reported in connection with it. And then always it would mysteriously disappear.

And countless persons must have dedicated their lives to the search for this Holy Grail, hoping in one way or another to partake of its sanctity and its awesome power. But here is a warning for you that you should take seriously, if you do go in search of the chalice. It always has been said that before approaching that grail one must purify oneself, undergo experiences of purification, for only the pure of spirit are likely to have any chance of finding it. And if anyone should happen to find it without first undergoing such purification, then the discovery of the chalice could be exceedingly dangerous.

Or you might seek another object of great power, a symbol or whatever it really is, that has always been called the Philosopher's Stone. The discovery of that stone has been the life-long objective of countless alchemists and others, and there are those who today still dedicate their lives to seeking it.

The stone is described as having the power to transmute base metals into gold, and it was believed that it did have that power, but that it also had much greater power than that. For in the notion of changing base metals into gold, is included the possibility of man's realizing all the potentials he possesses—powers that only are rumored, powers ordinarily attributed to gods, powers humanity has yet to dream about. And, in this trance, you may find yourself pursuing the legendary search for the Philosopher's Stone.

And there is also believed to be a very great mystery surrounding the Egyptian pyramids, the largest of those pyramids and, especially, the one that is known as the Great Pyramid. And built into that structure are believed to be innumerable mysteries and knowledge of a very high order that belonged to the most ancient and advanced civilizations, and about which we now know nothing.

There are secrets explaining how that pyramid was built, as its very existence cannot be explained on the basis of our present knowledge of what Egypt knew. But also many, many other secrets and items of knowledge of very great value, and it would be extremely beneficial for contemporary people to have access to that knowledge. So you might want to travel far, far back in time, or along whatever path opens to you, to try to fathom some of the secrets of that Great Pyramid.

And I will give you still one more mystery you might want to seek to penetrate when, in a little while, you and your coexplorer do begin your shared-trance voyage.

More and more as we learn about the past, it seems to us that there must have been civilizations far more ancient and more highly developed than any of which we now have knowledge or have been able to find any traces.

And there are countless myths to be encountered throughout the world about humanlike beings from some other planet or dimension or some other order of reality who brought to certain peoples of this earth the knowledge or means by which our first civilizations were able to arise.

Or rumors of mysterious objects deposited in a few locations on the earth, so that men discovering these became inspired and were enabled to advance much more quickly than evolution would have allowed them to do, and they created great civilizations, in some respects more sophisticated than our own. And these objects may have been venerated as gods, they may have been carried away in wars, or destroyed, or hidden away by civilizations facing destruction, so that some of those objects might still exist in some secret place, and there might be a few persons guarding that place, or perhaps no one knows any longer where those objects are hidden. But it might be possible to travel back through time, by means of images, and seek out the hidden or lost objects.

And you will believe, for the duration of the game, that all of these secrets and mysteries are real, and that the discoveries are possible.

And the pursuit of one of these legendary or mythic goals, or some similar goal, will be undertaken by you, two of you together, in the shared trance, and utilizing AMP, so that subjectively you will have months or even years in which to carry out your quest. And in terms of clock time, you will have one hour, all of the time you could ever want to have or be able to make use of.

You will go on that quest, and when it is over, and whether you have succeeded or failed, but when you have given it your very best efforts, and it is over, then one further task will await you.

For that task, you will have been strengthened by the journey of the spirit just completed, and that journey will have brought you much closer to the completion of this final task than anything else you could have done, and you will believe and know that this is true.

And your task will demand that you go deep together, going together very, very deep, down into the most profound psychic depths, down into regions of awareness that are cosmic, that are universal, and eternal. Going into those profound depths together, in a unique, shared adventure of the spirit, endeavoring together to arrive at and realize ultimate reality, some truly ultimate reality, in whatever form this apprehension may be experienced by you.

And this is a very, very serious undertaking, and you will approach it with a spirit of great seriousness, and knowing that in your joint exploration you are pioneers for all mankind, venturing along a new frontier. And you will undertake this with great respect for the psychic or other forces with which you may be dealing, but you will be confident that you are now as well prepared as you need be for the undertaking.

Those are your instructions, and you will remember them

in every detail. And now you will awaken and begin, in a moment, to induce altered states in one another, and deepening those states for one another, then coming together in the depths of trance, finding one another and proceeding from that point together.

And you will remember what you have learned from previous games. You will remember about signaling should you want to terminate trance, and about responding to the guide when the guide's hand is placed upon any player's shoulder.

You have one hour of clock time, with AMP, for the first stage of this game, and another hour, with AMP, for the second stage. And now begin the mutual induction and deepening.

Throughout, the guide will carefully observe the players, terminating any trances if requested, and at the end following the established procedure, terminating, first of all, the shared trance, establishing exclusive guide-player rapport, and then restoring each player to an alert, waking state.

When all trances have been terminated, the players will be instructed to make a very thorough record, both visual and verbal, of what happened during this game. Each player is to do this work alone, not consulting with the game partner or revealing to the partner what has been recorded.

The players may discuss what they have experienced with the guide, but not with anyone else, until the report has been completed.

At the next meeting of the group, the players may thoroughly discuss their respective experiences should they wish to do so.

Having given these instructions, the guide will once again caution the players against allowing shared-trance experiences to be a basis for emotional attachments.

Players will be asked to return to their homes and begin work at once on the written accounts of their sessions.

But any player who wishes to speak now with the guide, or to meditate on her or his experience, will remain.

## :: 12 ::

Should it have been successful on the earlier occasion, the players now will repeat, proceeding approximately as before, the experience of glossolalia, or speaking in tongues.

If that first effort is not regarded by the players as having been successful, and the guide thinks no second attempt to be warranted, then the players will omit this particular game and go on to do the next.

## :: 13 ::

Players will be asked to induce and deepen trance, and to go just as deeply into trance as they can go, and maximum depth will be signaled to both player and guide by an involuntary levitation to shoulder level of the player's right arm. When a player's arm has reached shoulder level, the guide will touch the extended hand of that player, and the arm will gently fall and the player will remain in trance, awaiting further instructions from the guide.

When all players have completed the deepening process, then the guide will say:

As I speak to you, you are going to find that you are going even deeper into trance, and you will just keep on going deeper, and let yourself keep going deeper throughout the playing of this extremely important mind game.

Listen to me with absolute attention, aware only of what I say to you, and of your own fulfilling of what is required of you by this game. And be certain that this game can be of the greatest benefit to you, and it could be the most important and beneficial of all the games you will play. In any case, it should be of major value for you.

And you know now that you are much more free than you were at the beginning of the first cycle of the games. You have access to capacities you could not draw upon before. And there are other capacities you have learned to use much more effectively than you could do before. Inhibitions and obstacles to creative thinking and work by now have been removed or diminished.

New possibilities have been opened to you. And all of this has made you more free and more completely yourself, and more fully human than you were before.

But still you remain less than completely free. And you are not yet entirely yourself. And no one can be considered fully human until the human potential has been very largely realized in that person.

And now you are going to be given an image, and it may be painful and frightening to you at first. But it also will be a very useful image, and a means by which you are going to achieve still greater freedom.

And I want you to go deeper, and to know and perceive that you are caught in the center, or near the center, of what looks like a giant spider's web.

There are many lines and threads of great strength that in different ways inhibit you or otherwise control you, and you see that they extend outward from your body, that you are caught in this web.

And these lines that entrap you and cripple you and impair you in so many ways are all symbolic forms referring back to persons or events from the past that still exert significant influence on you.

But I want you to know that these forces do not have to control you. That you have the possibility of really being free. And some of the lines of this web really have very little strength at all. They were strong once, but now they restrain you only because you are in the habit of being restrained by them, and do not really question their power.

And strike now at some of these lines, and you will see that some of them are easily broken. Strike them, and they will just snap or crumble. They were ready to be broken by you, and you don't even have to concern yourself as to where those lines came from or what they meant.

And now listen very carefully, and completely absorb and assimilate the truths that will be spoken to you. And you will know that the truth is being spoken, and you will incorporate everything acceptable to you into your own values system, into your most basic values system, on every level of your mind-body.

And know now that you are essentially free to use your body as you wish to use your body, so long as you use that body in what you yourself know to be an ethical way, with proper regard for other beings as well as for your own values. It is your body, and no one has the right to try to exercise controls over you in your body.

And you are free in your mind. You are free to think whatever thoughts you might want to think, to have whatever subjective experiences you might want to have. And no one has any right to exercise any dictatorial controls over what you do with your mind, and no right to impose guilt or any other penalties on you for your thoughts. And you are bound only by your own ethics and authentic responsibilities.

Know that your accomplishments are *your* accomplishments, they never can belong to anyone else. But you have been confused about this, and others have been confused about these matters of which I have been speaking to you.

There are people who have thought that your body was theirs to control. There are people who have thought that your mind was theirs to control. There are people who have thought that your accomplishments were their accomplishments, and they were confused and badly in error about that.

Yet they were able to confuse you, and to cause you to be in error about these matters too. But you do know now that you were in error, and you will not be in error about these matters any longer.

And you will understand now this web in which you are caught. It is very largely the product of such error and confusion, and being now free in your mind-body, and knowing that what you have accomplished is your accomplishment, strike out again at those lines, and smash through them.

And as you do this, becoming truly free from those forces that in the past have fettered you.

And now, if there are still lines remaining, go deeper and deeper and deeper into trance. I am going to give you five minutes of clock time, and that will be a very great amount of subjective, experiential time, and this is what you must do:

You will take note of each line still attached to you and

that has been unbreakable by you, and you will follow each one of those lines outward until you come to the source, the emanating point of the particular line. That source then will be revealed to you—the persons and experiences, whatever happened to create that particular line in the first place. And you will proceed to that source, and understand it, understanding with your present maturity, and destroying the power of that source, smashing the line that linked you to it.

In discovering these sources, these source-persons and events, you may discover that it was your own error that created the crippling line of influence which ever since has linked you to the past. Or you may discover that you were genuinely wronged by someone, and, if so, then it probably will be beneficial to you to express forgiveness, so that the past will not contain resentments or other strong negative feelings.

You will go to these sources, and cut through these lines, as often as need be, trying, if possible, to extricate yourself completely from the web. And in any case, becoming by this symbolic behavior on these very deep levels, much more free, more completely yourself, more fully human than you were before.

And you have that image of yourself in the web, and you know what it is that you must do, and you have been allotted time for this self-liberation, and you will begin it *now!*

At the end of this period, the guide will inquire if any player feels more time is needed, and will give more time if it is wanted. When all of the players have completed their task, to the extent they are able to complete it, then the guide will say:

You have gone to these sources, and you have understood certain things about experiences you have had, and about persons of importance in your life. You have learned about damage you have suffered, and sources of that damage.

Now, it may or may not be beneficial for you to remember all you have experienced during this exercise of setting yourself free. But we will leave that judgment to your own unconscious, so that you, when you have ended this trance, will remember all that you need to remember, and that you have no need not to remember, and you will forget anything you would not want to know or that it might be detrimental to you for you to know. And your own unconscious will determine what is to be remembered and what is to be forgotten. But whether you remember or forget, you will have achieved exactly the same liberation.

The guide then will terminate trances and will remind the players to make verbal and visual records of what they have experienced.

:: *14* ::

The guide will request the players to induce and deepen their own trances and to continue deepening the trance until the guide speaks to them again.

After five to ten minutes, the guide will say to the players:

And now go deeper and deeper, and on this occasion you should go very, very deep.

And find yourself now passing through that door which leads to the stone stairway, and this stairway is well known to you by now. And going down the stairs, and down, deeper and deeper, to where the black waters are, to where your boat is waiting.

Getting into that boat, and hearing the familiar lapping of the water, feeling the rocking, cradling motion as that boat carries you deeper and deeper. And this time, as that boat moves through the gloom, you will not proceed as you have done in the past.

You will not this time emerge into sunlight, but rather taking a different turn, and following a winding course through hewn passageways, caverns, going down deeper and deeper, and finally moving out into a large grotto, where around the circular edges of a lagoon or large pool each boat containing each player will come slowly to rest.

And look overhead now, and see that this place is very

beautifully lighted by moonlight coming down into the grotto through a long, cylindrical, carved-out opening in the stone. That moonlight is coming down to you from an opening far, far overhead, and you will know that the moonlight reaches down into this place through that aperture for only a very limited time, and rarely. It happens for a little less than an hour, and that only once each year, and this place where you are, this Grotto of the Moon, was created just so as to receive that particular moonlight at that particular time, and this is a sacred and magical place that was created very long ago.

And you have been brought here as a preparation for what you are going to experience as a culmination of the mind games.

Going deeper and deeper now, deeper and deeper, savor the mystery, and the enormous power of this place, this magical place, and listen to me very carefully now.

Before you can have the culminating experience toward which the mind games have been moving us, there are certain preparations you must make. And you will undertake those preparations during the coming week. At the end of that week, we will gather again, for the playing of the last mind game.

It is essential, in the coming week, that you take into your body just as little food as is required to maintain your health and strength. And that will be much less than you ordinarily take in. And you will not take into your body anything but plain and simple and nourishing substances.

You will not take into your body any kind of intoxicating substance, anything that would in any way affect your mental functioning.

You will try to maintain emotional serenity, keeping yourself free from emotional disturbances and from all excitement just as much as possible. It is of great importance that you maintain tranquillity in your mind and nervous system. And just to avoid any excitation, you should also refrain from any experiences leading to sexual arousal, or any kind of event that would be likely to lead to body-mind excitation.

You should approach the concluding mind game with a

mind that for the preceding week has been as nearly as possible like a calm, clear pool of water over which, ideally, not so much as a ripple passes. That is the ideal, and you will try to approach that ideal just as closely as possible, and you will experience that ideal now, going deeper and deeper and deeper, always going deeper with each word and image, and experiencing that calm, clear mind, so that you know what you must aim for.

And during the coming week of preparation, you will spend about one hour daily, not longer, inducing an altered state and deepening that state, going just as deep as you can. And on the first day, trying to follow your images, whatever images occur to you, having the intention of following the flow of those images, and of coming at last to some place where one goes beyond images, into whatever lies beyond images for you.

And doing this again, on the second and the third and the fourth days of the week, and on the fifth and sixth days having the aim of reaching the most profound and expanded awareness achievable by you in the deepest trance you are able to attain. But not then in any way analyzing or otherwise thinking about what happened as a result of that intention. Because what happens in those trances could easily be misunderstood by you, and what happens in those trances almost surely will not have a meaning comprehensible to you, but will refer in some veiled, symbolic way to matters of which you have no knowledge.

It is also very likely that after those trances you will spontaneously forget what occurred, and if you do not, then you should put out of your mind what happened and not permit yourself to think about the content of those trances at all.

And you will, on the day preceding our final gathering, place yourself once again in isolation. This time you will not fast, but will eat very lightly. You will drink water only, and you will sleep just as much as you find yourself inclined to sleep. And you will spend that twenty-four hours relaxing, sleeping, inducing and deepening trances, and waiting with gathering anticipation for your participation in the game you will play on the following day.

And this final isolation period will be started by you at about six o'clock in the evening, and you will end it so as to be able to arrive at the place where the game is to be played at exactly seven o'clock, proceeding directly there from the place where you have been.

And all players must understand that once the final game has begun there can be no interruptions, and to prevent this the door to the place of games will be locked and cannot be opened again until the game has ended.

But should a player be unable to reach the place of the game before it is sealed, then that player should know that she or he will be given an opportunity to play the culminating game, but will have to play it individually instead of with the group.

The guide will enable you to have that experience, and you will not under any circumstances be deprived of that opportunity. Having come so far, it is your right which you have earned, and that right will be respected.

Going deeper and deeper now, going deeper and noting that over your head the moonlight is fading. It soon will be total darkness here.

And you are aware only of yourself now, only of yourself and your responses to my words, and you will feel that your boat is moving, moving on back through the winding caverns, back toward that shore from which you started.

Coming back and back, until you find yourself at that starting place, that place at the bottom of the stone stairs, and getting out of the boat now, and climbing up those stairs, and, as you climb them, experiencing yourself as emerging from the trance.

Feeling your trance becoming lighter and lighter as you come closer to the top of the stairs, and you are almost completely awake, and you are at the top of the stairs, already feeling very refreshed, and passing on through the door now and eyes opening and *wide awake!*

:: *15* ::

The guide will welcome the players and will request that altered states be self-induced and deepened. An involuntary right-arm levitation will indicate when maximum depth has been reached, and the guide then will touch the player's hand, and the arm will lower, and the player will remain in deep trance until the guide speaks again.

When all players are ready to proceed, the guide will say:

And now you will come with me once again, for one last time, as we play the mind games, to that door through which on occasion you have passed and have then found yourself standing alone at the top of a massive stone stairway.

You are standing there now, but, as your trance deepens, you find to your bewilderment that the stairway is much longer, and goes down much deeper than you recalled it to go, or ever have observed it to go on past occasions.

Proceeding down now, down those stairs, going deeper and deeper, you notice that the stairway continues far, far down, as far as you can see into the darkness, so that you can't even see where those stairs go and end.

And, as you keep going down and down, you are going deeper and deeper into trance, down and down and down the stairs, and still not perceiving any end, but moving forward now into the darkness that rises around you, as you still keep going deeper and deeper, and now, as you still are going deeper and deeper, feeling more and more sure of your footing, until finally you know that you now are at the bottom of the stairs.

And listening only to my voice, aware now of nothing but my voice, not of any place or time, or of your body, not aware of anything at all but the sound of my voice, and not aware very much of who is listening to the voice that is speaking, and not concerned with who it is speaking to you. There is just a voice, there is just experience, and there is the experience now of the question.

And just becoming aware of the question, the question you are beginning to ask without thinking that it is you who are asking, but aware of the question: *Who am I?* And of the series of concentric circles, meditated on by you before. And the question, addressed to the outer circle, and the image of a symbol arising in response, symbol of the outer, most superficial personality in its concern with the most ordinary activities and goals of everyday life.

And going deeper by addressing each circle, as the circles move inward toward the center, and each time receiving a symbol that is deeper and also more comprehensive, a symbol representing more and more of the whole person, and more and more of the whole life of the person, a symbol expressing the person more and more profoundly, and going deeper and deeper now, repeating the question, *Who am I? Who am I?*

And the question reverberating down and down, until finally you will reach the center, the innermost circle, asking *Who am I?* And then you will maintain that depth of trance and that image of the innermost circle, as your head very slowly falls forward, maintaining that trance and that image until you are spoken to again.

The guide, when all players have made that response, will say:

And now, looking at that innermost circle, meditate on it, and with absolute intensity and seriousness inquire: *Who am I?*

*Who am I?* And there will arise into consciousness now an image of the deepest and most comprehensive self-symbol yet realized by you. The deepest and most comprehensive symbol of the self as the self now is.

And you will hold that symbol before you, achieving that symbol, holding that symbol, and having it, and holding it, you will remain very, very deeply in trance, and your head will slowly, involuntarily resume an upright position.

The guide will wait for these responses to be made and then will say to the players:

And now, going deeper and deeper, and keeping that symbol before you as you go, and being drawn down, and down, into that symbol, and being one with that symbol that is you, yourself contained and represented in that symbol, know that you have reached that moment we have been moving toward, and the moment when you are going to die.

The moment when you will and must die, and after that you will be reborn.

And this is one of the great sacred mysteries, experienced by peoples of this planet since the most remote times of which we have knowledge.

You have come a very long way to reach this point. You have gained many strengths and you have overcome certain weaknesses, but there are significant weaknesses and problems that do still remain.

And I now address that symbol which is you, and advise you that, dying, you may be free, and leave behind your problems and weaknesses that you have, so that when you are reborn, you will retain your strengths, retaining what you would want to retain, bringing that back into the world with you, but leaving behind you much that you would want to leave behind. And you *are* that symbol, that deep, comprehensive symbol, completely identified now with that symbol, in these last moments preceding the death of the self as that symbol represents it, represents you.

Perceive that symbol clearly now, and become aware that the symbol is becoming smaller and smaller. And know, as that symbol grows smaller and smaller, before it is extinguished altogether, that when that symbol is extinguished, then you will die.

You will die as your old self, and will remain in death, the death of that self, for as long as needs to be, so that there can occur whatever transformations of the self are going to occur, before you can be born again.

The symbol becoming now smaller and smaller, as you near the moment of the self's extinction, and as you near the moment of death, and knowing that the symbol is dwindling down to the tiny point preceding its extinction, and the moment at which you will die.

And the last thing you will hear before dying, and the first thing you will know later on, is that after the experience of rebirth, you will open your eyes and behold the world as it is in that moment when you are born again.

And now, that symbol going finally out, the self extinguished, now in the moment of your death.

The guide will observe the players very closely, but without interfering with any person's experience unless there are extremely urgent reasons why this should be done. And the guide will know that it is to be expected that this can be an emotionally very powerful experience, and that the most powerful experiences usually are also the most beneficial.

The guide also will know that the death experiences can be of greatly varying duration, and that these often will take a player into depths of trance so profound that no longer will the guide be able to communicate with that player. The guide must not be anxious or fearful about this, and must allow every player adequate time to go through, in the player's own way, the symbolic death and rebirth.

And after the rebirth experience has occurred, the guide should take the hand of each player, and say: "Look around you now, all around. And get up and move around, and touch, and smell, and experience your world completely, and allow yourself all the time you might want to savor this state which you are in now, this state just after being born again."

The players then should be free to speak to one another, to do anything they might wish to do, except that it must be required that the players will remain in the place where the game is being played.

And when it seems appropriate to do so, the guide will ask the players to regroup, and the guide will inquire if all players are awake, or whether it will be required to terminate trances, and the guide will accept the players' responses to these questions.

The guide then will ask the players to go singly or together, as they may choose, except that any player who feels in need of talking with the guide or an assistant guide will remain for that purpose.

And in parting, the guide will congratulate each player,

and suggest that all players soon agree upon a meeting at which time the possible future of that group will be decided.

And finally, the guide will remain in that place alone (no longer in the role of guide), with the player who will perform the guiding function during the former guide's own experience of death and rebirth.

And with that, the mind games are concluded.

*Guide's Book for Mind Games*

# A Special Note to Mind-Games Players:

The "Guide's book for mind games" supplements
instruction implicit and explicit in the other four books
of the games. It is a valuable aid and must be read before
guiding of the games is attempted, but it cannot be a
complete manual providing instructions for each and every
situation.

Guides, with the basic information provided, must learn
by doing. Eventually, there should be available many
experienced guides to advise the new, learning guides, but
that is not presently the case.

For now, guides and players are explorers, learning
together, probing new frontiers. Perfection is not at all to
to be expected, but major errors will be avoided if this
book and the preceding books are carefully studied and
thought about.

Guiding is an ancient and honorable role, and the guide
re-emerges now, at a critical point in human history,
to perform services never more urgently or more profoundly needed.

Every Mind-game guide should know this, meditate
upon it, and be guided.

## 1

Having studied the games and considered the task well, the guide should share with the players certain beliefs, understandings, expectations, and wishes important to the outcome of the playing of the games:

Mind games anticipate the play-learning systems of the future, opening that future *now*.

Mind games are education, ecstasy, entertainment, self-exploration, powerful instruments of growth.

Those who play these games should become more imaginative, more creative, more fully able to gain access to their capacities and to use their capacities more productively.

The players should achieve a new image of man as a creature of enormous and unfolding potentials.

The players should become, *by their own experience*, increasingly hopeful that the powers of the human being are sufficient to deal with the problems that confront us.

The players should emerge from these games convinced that man is not something we know has to be surpassed; rather, man still is something to be realized—and is realizable.

And the mind games are a means of advancing toward what must be the main goal of every person in our time— *putting the first man on the earth.*

## 2

With the help of the guide, the players will learn to alter and expand consciousness. By this alteration and expansion, new ways of knowing and being will be experienced and explored.

Players will use a pragmatic model of consciousness as a vast continuum of *states of consciousness,* many of these states lying far beyond the present experience of any player. Along this continuum and through these states, it is demonstrably possible to move, into dimensions and types of awareness still little and in some cases almost wholly unexplored.

With the help of the guide, the players will learn that what is sometimes called "normal waking consciousness" is only a very limited area, comprising just a small range of states along the continuum. And within that range, still thought of as "normal," players will learn that only a few of their capacities are accessible to them, and even those can be used only partially.

The guide will enable the players to experience expansions of consciousness, movements along the continuum, and the resulting access to more and more of the players' potentials.

Players will learn self-regulation of consciousness, and, with this, will perceive that it is possible to expand the *general norms* of consciousness, to enrich the experience and capacities of *all* human beings.

And the guide will point out that this general expansion must expand the entire reality consensus—making the whole human reality deeper, broader, much more multidimensional, and richer, until we will one day look back astounded at the impoverished world of consciousness we once shared, and supposed to be the real world—our officially defined and defended "*reality*."

:: 3 ::

Mind games should be played only by those who freely choose to participate, and who feel well motivated to do so.

In general, the games may be played by anyone sufficiently mature and intelligent to understand why the games are being played, to be able to respond to the demands of the games, and to be able to make the personal, free decision to be a participant. In deciding to play, a player should understand that achievements will depend upon who is playing, especially a person's potentials, life experience, motivation, and the efforts that are made.

Children will not ordinarily have the needed maturity and

understandings to be able to make an adequate response to the games. There should and must be mind games for persons of all ages, including small children, and in the near future such mind games will be routine in education at all levels. Present mind games will help to make clear how much of the mind is left untouched by ordinary educational procedures.

:: 4 ::

Groups of players should probably number not less than five or more than eleven for the games to be played most effectively. And there should be an odd number of participants, since some mind games are played by couples, while one member of the group is acting as the guide.

The guide will be chosen by members of the group, and it is highly desirable that the choice of the guide be unanimous. In the mind games, there is no place for conflict or "encounter," and groups will find it difficult to function without an unusual degree of harmony, sharing of purposes, and rapport between all players.

Especially at the beginning of the games, the guide will have to be effective at enabling players to experience ASCs, or trances. The guide must be able to induce these states, and must teach self-induction by the players themselves. The guide must be able to deepen the trances, and must teach the players to self-deepen trances.

From the beginning, the guide will provide suggestions and structure the playing of the games in such a way that the experiencing of the games is an expression of the individuality of each player.

Groups must avoid the error: Guide = Leader. The role of the guide is to be understood by everyone as that of the one who assists, the one who enables.

The guide is the enabler, the one who opens the gateways, and who then serves the needs of the games and of the players.

:: 5 ::

At the beginning, a guide will be selected who is well able to induce and deepen trances, and whose judgment, intelligence, knowledge, and empathy are respected by the players. It will be valuable if this guide has had a long-standing interest in the kinds of experiences with which the mind games are concerned. The guide should be a good practical psychologist, able to establish good rapport with the players, and should be self-confident, but not overconfident, about his or her ability to carry out the guiding tasks.

Eventually, during the four mind-games cycles, as many players as possible should have the experience of guiding, and all players as they experience the games will become better qualified by that experience to act as guides. But, in the beginning, the guide must be chosen by the group with particular care. Probably, several persons will be tested in a preliminary session, as to their capacity to induce and deepen ASCs and to guide the experience of players once the states have been induced.

In general, guides should have the ability to make very close observation of others, and to communicate lucidly and be able to say exactly what she or he intends to say.

The guide should be alert to nonverbal communications, being able to receive these and also to utilize gestures, facial expressions, and other, less obvious nonverbal means of communicating to the players.

And especially the guide must rehearse and plan out the inductions and deepenings and other instructions to the players, learning to use the voice to elicit maximum responses, conveying feelings and subtle suggestions in addition to the more obvious information content.

The guide must repeatedly practice ahead of a session the verbal instructions to be given, and also should imagine varieties of possible situations that might arise while a game is being played, so being well prepared for the objective situations by the experienceing of the imagined, subjective ones.

However, the guide will always react to the players in the actual session, being assisted but never bound by the imaginative preparations and rehearsals.

## :: 6 ::

Valuable background knowledge for the guide will be found in the literatures of hypnosis, psychedelic experience, mythology, art, the creative process, religion and the religious experience, yoga, zen, and other spiritual disciplines, and psychology and psychiatry as these objectively or fairly deal with creativity, the imagination, and the experiencing of altered states of consciousness by normal persons for experimental or other sound purposes.

Narrow, pathology-oriented psychological and psychiatric approaches to ASC phenomena should be considered irrelevant.

## :: 7 ::

All guides should read, reread, and thoroughly assimilate information contained in the following books:

Jay Haley (Ed.), *Advanced Techniques of Hypnosis and Therapy: Selected Papers of Milton H. Erickson, M.D.* Grune & Stratton: New York, 1967.

Linn F. Cooper and Milton H. Erickson, *Time Distortion in Hypnosis.* Williams & Wilkins: Baltimore, 1959.

R. E. L. Masters and Jean Houston, *The Varieties of Psychedelic Experience.* Holt, Rinehart & Winston: New York, 1966. Paperback edition. Delta: New York, 1967.

If these books are not available in bookstores, they should be obtained directly from the publishers. Groups will want the volumes available for reference, and they should be made the nucleus of a small mind-games library.

The authors hope to have available to players a phonograph record which should be invaluable in illustrating induction, deepening, and a variety of guiding procedures.

When published, the authors' book, *New Ways of Being,* will detail the experimental work underlying the mind games, and will give much further information of value to guides and players.

## :: 8 ::

Guides will always need to be alert against using mind games as a vehicle for their own "ego trips."

And the players, should it become necessary, will assist the guide's avoidance of improper attitudes by means of constructive criticism and humor.

Before each game, the person who is guide will prepare for the guiding task by a period of relaxation, deep breathing, and meditation. This meditation will be used by the guide especially to become conscious of, and eliminate, ego hungers and power drives, other improper attitudes and cravings, and any tendencies to be exploitative or self-servingly manipulative of the mind-games players.

Each guide will determine her or his own needs, and prepare the meditations accordingly.

Players should wish for the guide to be self-regulating in these matters.

If necessary, players will provide criticism, tactfully, and with a high regard for preserving harmony within the group.

Players should know that the guide requires their confidence and cooperation to function effectively.

It is in the players' interest to give these whenever possible.

## :: 9 ::

There always will be two assistant guides, both selected by the group, or one selected by the group and one by the principal or first guide.

These assistants will be available to serve in the first guide's absence, or in games where more than one guide may be wanted.

Also, one of these assistants will serve as guide to the first guide, so that the first guide will be able to experience most mind games as a player also. The first guide will, of course, miss participation in those games which all group members play together simultaneously and all interacting (such as the Group-Spirit games, and the creation of collective works of art).

234

But it should be considered of first importance that the guide experience each game also as a player whenever that is possible.

:: *10* ::

When a group has been formed, there should be preliminary meetings to select the first guide and assistants, and also to determine settings for the games, and to correct any misunderstandings and improper orientations any players might have.

These preliminary meetings also may reveal persons who for one reason or another should not be allowed to continue with the group. These persons then will be disqualified, on grounds that might be disruptiveness, unethical conduct, or obvious inability to play the games.

It should be understood that it is extremely important that when a group is formed, only those persons be accepted as members who are likely to continue to participate until the games are finished.

It will be most disruptive, especially in smaller groups, if one or more persons should decide to drop out of the games.

If a player should have to withdraw, however, or a player has to be disqualified, then it will not be an advisable procedure, unless at the very outset, to try to find a replacement. Rather, the group will have to continue with a smaller number of players.

:: *11* ::

Before the first game is started, the players will have discussed the games' general and over-all content.

All players will have at least some notion of how the games are developed in the mind-games books, and the guide will have made a thorough study of the books in advance of this discussion of the content.

It should be a stated goal of the group that a main purpose of the games is to allow the person to function more effectively within the reality consensus, in the "external world," and according to the legitimate demands of everyday life.

This in no way precludes the goal of a general as well as a personal expansion of consciousness.

Players will agree to approach their forthcoming experiences without superstition or credulousness, and to take precautions against overvaluing any particular experience. It is not usually a particular game experience that will be of major importance, but the over-all impact of the games—the learning, the growth, the liberation of potentials, the achievements resulting from the playing through of the entire mind-games cycle.

It will be agreed that each mind game, upon completion, should be looked at critically, and the rational faculties of the mind be brought to bear upon the game experience and any apparent consequences. Players should place high value on this criticism, as what the group is working toward is a higher creative synthesis and harmonious working together of reason with imagination, a better balance and more complete working together of the mind-brain, of the complete mind-body system, and of the whole person.

It should be noted that fantastic images and experiences will be encountered repeatedly by the mind-games players, because these are especially stimulating and nourishing to the imagination, the creative process, and factors affecting creativity, motivation, and liberated potentials. And we are working in these mind games to achieve, as one of our primary goals, the freer expression in the player of originality and creative imagination. These have been among the most neglected of the person's capacities, and especially need to be exercised, productively applied, and integrated on the conscious level.

Players should know before hand what is being aimed for and being done, and that they are going to have some experiences of a kind that in the past often have been regarded with superstitious awe, and otherwise overvalued in both negative and positive ways.

The mind games deal with known experiential capacities of the human being, and they are directed toward using these capacities to realize potentials of the person and to make that person at once more fully realized, more fully human, and more free. *The games are not the expression of any religion, spiritual discipline, occult or other belief-system, or of any ideology apart from the general aims stated.*

*The games will only be diluted and distorted should an attempt be made to narrow their scope, and make them serve the purposes of any particular doctrine or ideology.*

Thus the players should know and fully understand that their mind-games experiences cannot decide, for example, anything about the reality or ontological status of worlds of images, or intelligent nonhuman life forms experienced as symbolic forms and images in a particular game.

When this is understood, the players will be better able to evaluate experiences they or others may have. And the mind games should not infect anyone with credulousness or superstition, *but rather should provide a good measure of immunization against these.*

The games also, however, should encourage players not to accept too constricted a reality, or arbitrary norms for consciousness, but to push for expansions of awareness, and for continuous explorations of the contents and processes of mind.

:: *12* ::

The players will consider at a preliminary meeting the necessity for having settings most conducive to the successful playing of the games.

The games will be played, for the most part, indoors, and the setting should be one that is comfortable, aesthetically pleasing, and as free as possible from any distractions. Children and animals must be excluded. Distracting noises from the street or from within a building should be as minimal as possible, and the players should take precautions against such disruptions as the ringing of a telephone or the arrival of unexpected persons, or of persons not mind-games players.

It has to be agreed that these games must be played with only the guide and players present. The games cannot be played satisfactorily with friends or other spectators present.

If it is wished by the group to demonstrate some game to persons not members of the group, then this should be a game already successfully played, and the demonstration should be quite apart from the regular playing of that game.

If possible, the same setting should be used for all or most occasions, especially if a very comfortable and secluded setting has been found. The environment then will be at once least intrusive on the experience of the players, and there will be created a climate most conducive to easy entry into, and deepening of, altered states of consciousness.

It should also be called to the players' attention that there are going to be several occasions when each player will need to be able to go into total isolation. The players should provide well ahead of time for such a place.

Similarly, the players should plan ahead of time for the out-of-doors locations they might want to use from time to time according to their own wishes, or as specified by the mind-games books.

The players should take very seriously this matter of a comfortable, distraction-free environment or setting for the playing of the games, since the failure to provide such a setting can be extremely detrimental to the results obtained, and may even lead to the collapse of the effort to play the games.

:: 13 ::

The guide and others will work out well in advance certain practical details involved in the playing of some of the games.

For example, it occasionally will be necessary to choose and obtain art materials with which the group will be working.

Music is required for some of the games, and the guide must very carefully consider the intended response and then select, perhaps with the help of some qualified player, music that will best enable that particular group to obtain the desired effects. Since the choice of music may vary greatly, depending upon the composition of a group, no recommendations will be made.

With regard to the art materials, decisions will include

whether to create drawings only, or possibly paintings and sculptures, or some other kinds of works of art. Qualified players will help make these decisions, and will select the materials that are needed.

:: *14* ::

The frequency with which mind games are to be played will have to be determined by the needs and wishes of a particular group. But, as a general rule, the best progress is likely to be made when the games are played not less often than once each week, and not more often than three times each week.

On the other hand, some particular group might find its own progress best facilitated by a greater or a lesser frequency. And, while this has not as yet been tested, it might be possible to move through the games in an intensive, accelerated way, in a retreat situation of the type used by the Jesuits for the Ignatian exercises.

Should an intensive retreat be attempted, then the responses of the players should be observed with particular care, so that no one is pushed too hard or too far. The completion of the mind games within a period of, say, thirty days, will call for careful scheduling and other planning, and a high degree of cooperation from everyone concerned.

:: *15* ::

It is of the greatest importance that the guide examine very carefully the language of the mind-games books, and especially the language that is given to be spoken directly to the players.

The guide should practice reading aloud and speaking this language, and should practice especially the inductions and the deepening procedures until these can be given lucidly, with confidence, and without hesitation. The words must flow easily, and the guide must know that what is being said is exactly what the guide wants to say.

The language of the mind-games inductions has been based upon careful observation and research into how to speak to persons in altered states of consciousness, how to talk to a person to alter consciousness, and how to speak to the unconscious mind and to the whole body of the person. And we sometimes refer to this kind of language or speech as "subcortical linguistics," although that term is, of course, more suggestive than precise.

The guide and players will gradually learn this way of speaking, and how best to receive these kinds of communications. Reading the mind-games books, observe the sinuousness of this language, that there are undulating, flowing movements, a circularity, a careful meandering, not words that are choppy, or words that go marching in a straight line like drilling soldiers.

We have learned that the more autonomous, imaginative mind of the ASCs, prefers to be talked to in that more sinuous way, that almost caressing way, and is more responsive to that kind of approach.

The guide must also painstakingly practice and observe the effects of different kinds of intonation, speaking, for example, so that an emphasis is placed always upon exactly what ought to be emphasized, and the voice sometimes will be most effective if it is somewhat monotonous, apart from the emphasis placed upon the most important words or phrases. But each guide must learn from experience, and for herself or himself.

:: 16 ::

The guide, in inducing and deepening trances, will want to slightly modify the given language, so as to be completely comfortable in it. However, extensive modifications should not be attempted until a guide has become fairly skilled in induction, deepening, and other aspects of guiding.

In making a study of the language of the games, the guide will find that often there is a progressive engagement of imageries in all sensory modalities of the mind-games players. And this is calculatedly done for a variety of reasons.

By suggesting to a player something for her to see, something for her to hear, to touch, to smell, and to taste, and by suggesting to her bodily movements, one simultaneously deepens her trance and gives her the means to function normally within the subjective reality.

When these things have been done for the player, she has open to her all kinds of experiences, and then her role-taking is facilitated, her sense of real participation grows, and as this happens the ASC deepens further, until the player may reach a profoundly altered state with full experiencing of the imaginal world or other subjective reality to be explored.

## :: 17 ::

The guide and the players should understand that there will be considerable individual differences in depth of trance and in capacities to respond to particular suggestions or carry out particular tasks.

Players who do not at first go into trance, or who have some doubts about whether they respond, should be asked to vividly imagine that they are in trance, and then to respond as they are inclined to respond.

All players should be told that they will learn to respond better and better as the games progress, that every player will improve with practice.

However, there always will be individual differences with respect to game performance, as there are differences between the players otherwise, and any one player will succeed more completely in some of the games than another player will, and in other games will do less well than the other player will.

The guide must make certain that there is no competition between the players about such matters as depth of trance, or quality of imagery.

Consciousness and phenomena must not be hierarchized or made the means of acquiring status.

Each player's progress or lack of progress is an entirely personal matter, measurable only in terms of the previous capacities of that player.

## :: 18 ::

While much may be accomplished with mildly altered states, it is always desirable that each player develop a capacity to alter consciousness profoundly, or go into very deep trances.

The reason for this is that, as a rule, the more profound the alteration, the more faculties or capacities to which the person is able to gain access.

Some of these capacities will be so firmly inhibited that they may be disinhibited *only* when there is a very deep trance or other profoundly altered state. However, once the access has been gained, and the person knows about and has used the capacity, then there may occur a diminishment of the inhibition, so that later on the ASC may not have to be so extreme.

Very deep trances also usually allow more effective use of the capacities of the person, and in deep trance the player should be able to concentrate better, to have better access to memories and learnings, to have richer images and externalize the images, to work more effectively with AMP, and to activate deep-lying or heavily obstructed growth-promoting dynamisms and processes.

Without the deep trances, at the very least the progress is likely to be slower.

For these reasons, and others the games will make apparent, all players and the guide should aim for the deepest possible trances, the most profound ASCs.

Having the capacity to achieve these deep trances, then the guide and players will utilize that capacity or not depending upon the particular game and the particular objectives.

:: 19 ::

The guide will give particular attention and thought to those mind-games exercises teaching players how to deal with menacing images or other unpleasant situations that might occasionally arise for some player or players.

The guide will remember that the person who is having an experience is in a suggestible state and may be rather easily diverted from any painful or threatening images and ideas. This often can best be done by appealing to the preference of the ASC mind for a kind of logic and behavior more characteristic of fairy tales or myths or legends, than of the every-day world of ordinary states of consciousness.

Guides might also have to deal on occasion with the reluctance of some player to be aroused from the altered state. And there may be occasions when a player will not communicate with the guide or acknowledge receiving any communication from the guide.

The guide should know, first of all, that any person in a trance will always emerge from that trance, so that there is no reason whatever to become anxious about the trance not terminating.

Anyone in trance not aroused from the trance will eventually just go to sleep, and then awaken back into that person's ordinary waking state. But it may be inconvenient if a player will not terminate trance when requested to do so, or will not communicate or acknowledge awareness of the guide.

Confronted by unwillingness to communicate, the guide will want to inquire if the player is having an experience the player does not want to have interrupted, and the guide may say that if this is the case and the player does not want to speak, then the player could just indicate awareness of the guide by means of some body movement.

The guide might request that the body of the player give an answer without the player's mind being distracted, so that the player will not at all have to think about either the question or the answer. For example, the left hand may involuntarily rise if the answer is *yes*, or the right hand if the answer is *no*. Or, if the player does not respond to this verbal request, then the guide may make physical contact with the player, and might say:

I am going to take your hand now, and then I'm going to close the fingers of that hand. And if you are aware of what I am saying, and do not wish to be disturbed for a while, then just slowly straighten out your fingers, and move your hand a little from one side to the other. And I will speak to you later on.

Or the guide may improvise other means, but in any case the guide should not become alarmed about a player's declining to communicate or to terminate a trance always at the guide's request.

The guide will also encounter a few players who on occasion do not completely awaken from trance when the usual suggestions for waking are given. Those players then should be given additional instructions and countings, until they feel themselves wide awake.

:: *20* ::

Refusals to come out of trance or communicate, also may be tactics of attention-seekers and "psychic exhibitionists," who sometimes turn up in a group.

These persons will also engage in other disruptive behaviors, and will tend to introduce competitiveness as well as distraction into the games.

If these persons will not halt disruptive activities, then there is no choice but to drop them from the group.

:: *21* ::

Group members, during the playing of these games, will often come to feel an unusual closeness to one another, and they may feel especially drawn together by the extraordinary experiences they share.

However, it is an important task of the guide to insist that the players maintain their usual contacts outside the group, and it should never be permitted to occur that the group becomes cultic, exclusive, an elitist in-group type of subculture, or anything of that sort.

:: *22* ::

The mind games emphatically are not intended to be played by any persons who are being affected by mind-altering drugs.

It certainly will be detrimental to the progress of the group as a whole if individual players are making use of substances to differentiate their experiences from those of the group.

Moreover, the mind games are means by which, without

any chemical or mechanical aids, players become able to alter consciousness and to conduct inner-space explorations, gaining access to and use of potentials, and otherwise extending the range of experiences available to people using only their natural capacities.

The authors, as veteran researchers with psychedelics, appreciate the value of those substances under certain conditions and have made this appreciation known in books and other writings.

But the mind games, and this needs to be repeated, should not be played by persons being influenced by psychedelics or any other mind-changing substances.

For some players, we will add, the mind games may well be a means of ending their dependence upon psychoactive chemicals as a means for getting at their blocked potentials.

:: 23 ::

The guides, and any others chosen by the group, should be available to players who feel the need to discuss experiences they have had in the games.

Players may want to ask advice about how to understand these experiences, about how to play the games better, about how to integrate some of the mind-games experiences, or some other kind of advice.

And in each group of players, persons willing and best qualified to listen and to give such advice will be designated.

If these persons are not the current guides, then they should inform the first guide of any matters bearing on the guiding of the games, or which they feel the current guide should know.

:: 24 ::

The role of the guide is more ancient than history, and it is no less important today than at any time in the past.

In playing the mind games, every player has the right to assume that the guide feels that role to be challenging, demanding, and of great importance, so that each person will give his or her best efforts to the task.

For the guide, the performance of this task should be regarded as a means of learning communications and leadership skills that will be of great value to the person for the remainder of that person's life.

Guiding, as from times immemorial, has applications in every sphere of the person's daily existence.

And it leads us into realms as yet unfathomed, out of which may emerge more completely human new ways of being.